PENGUIN ANANDA
THE MAGIC OF FRIENDSHIPS

Shubha Vilas is a TEDx speaker, a lifestyle coach, a storyteller and an author. He studied patent law after completing his engineering degree but finally chose the path of a spiritual seeker.

Ramayana: The Game of Life is his bestselling series. He's also the author of *Open-Eyed Meditations*, *Mystical Tales for a Magical Life* and *Perfect Love: 5.5 Ways to a Lasting Relationship*. The focus of his work is the application of scriptural wisdom to day-to-day life and addressing the needs of corporates and the youth through thought-provoking seminars.

He has delivered more than 4000 talks, inspiring more than 5,25,000 people, across ten countries in last ten years. He is also a visiting faculty at several premiere business management schools in India including the Indian Institute of Management (IIM), and Narsee Monjee Institute of Management Studies (NMIMS), Mumbai. He has also been a guest speaker at the prestigious Massachusetts Institute of Technology (MIT), Boston; Dresden International University, Germany; University of the Witwatersrand (WITS), Johannesburg; and several centres of Indian Institute of Technology in India.

He travels across the globe couselling and guiding students on leadership, overcoming failures and managing stress, among other concerns.

To know more about him, visit www.shubhavilas.com.

The **MAGIC**

of **FRIENDSHIPS**

Understand it
Cherish it, Keep it

★

Shubha Vilas

PENGUIN
ANANDA
An imprint of Penguin Random House

PENGUIN ANANDA

USA | Canada | UK | Ireland | Australia
New Zealand | India | South Africa | China

Penguin Ananda is part of the Penguin Random House group of companies
whose addresses can be found at global.penguinrandomhouse.com

Published by Penguin Random House India Pvt. Ltd
7th Floor, Infinity Tower C, DLF Cyber City,
Gurgaon 122 002, Haryana, India

First published in Penguin Ananda by Penguin Random House India 2020
Copyright © Shubha Vilas 2020

10 9 8 7 6 5 4 3 2 1

The views and opinions expressed in this book are the author's own and the facts
are as reported by him which have been verified to the extent possible, and the
publishers are not in any way liable for the same.

ISBN 9780143446552

Typeset in Adobe Caslon Pro by Manipal Technologies Limited, Manipal
Printed at Thomson Press India Ltd, New Delhi

www.penguin.co.in

To Vibhav, Azhar, Lenin, Dibin, Sydney, Rohan, Akshay, Shubhapriya, Sonia, Amareta, Valerie and Alzira from my formative years; to Radheshlal, Rajgopal, Shadbhuj, and the thousands of friends from across the world who considered me worthy of friendship!

To all my readers

Contents

1

Friendship Should Bring Joy

Dos and Don'ts of Friendship

I meet several youngsters every day. One of the things I have realized after these meetings is that friendships play a critical role in shaping your life and your future. They are more important than even parents and teachers in setting the course and the speed of your progress.

Let me begin by telling you a story from my own life. When I was in the fourth grade, I was admitted to one of the best private schools in Goa. I was born and raised in a middle-class Indian family where my basic needs were met, but there was no scope for luxuries, and so this school proved to be a difficult choice for my parents. However, since my father was keen that I get the best education, he paid through his nose to get me into that school and continued to pay the steep fees. But that was it. There was no other way you could compare me to any of the students, who arrived in long, gleaming cars and had many other luxuries at their disposal. The result was that even though I was studying in the most sought-after school in the state, I was miserable. I did not have a single friend who could understand my predicament or sympathize with me. Far from it, in fact—all I got to hear were sarcastic remarks from my fellow students. I developed a massive complex. My confidence level plummeted. I couldn't remember anything I studied. My teachers branded me 'dull' and 'below average'. To worsen it all, my classmates wouldn't even allow me to play with them because I wasn't one of them (whatever that *really* meant!).

Finally, my parents decided to pull me out of the school, not that they had a choice at that point: the school had already warned them that they would hold me back in the same grade if I stayed, which none of us wanted. So I was admitted to an all-boys' public school. Things immediately seemed different. I no longer had the luxury of studying in a class of just twenty; this school was overcrowded and bursting with students. Even the football team had a strength of at least fifty players per game. There were so many boys kicking the ball that more often than not, the ball was hardly visible!

At first, I felt lost in the crowd and wondered if we had made the right choice. But soon, in the maddening crowd, I found two gems: two boys in my class who changed me and my destiny completely! One was a sports hero—in cricket and football—and the other was a thinker, while I was just the shy, unconfident guy. But the three of us struck up a friendship like no other. My confidence swelled just from being in their company. In less than a year, I was not just clearing my exams but topping the class—all thanks to the two friends who helped me find myself.

I also learnt that this was not a unique experience. Several well-known leaders from across the globe have talked about how friendships have helped them change and grow and how they are who they are because of their friends.

Studies have revealed that most modern problems, such as depression, drug addiction, divorce, obesity and even suicidal tendencies, are connected to friendship. Shocking, isn't it? Let me tell you the story of Ramsey, who is an example of this point I'm trying to make. I met Ramsey when I was conducting a private study—not restricted to any country—to explore the prominent emotion that drove the youth to obesity, specifically in the age group of eighteen to twenty-four years. He was twenty at the time and was probably the most obese youngster I had ever met. It took him considerable effort to just stand up and shake my hand. Even before I began to talk to him, I empathized with his situation. I shuddered to imagine what he would face in college, especially because he was going to one of the most happening colleges in the city, which was also notorious for 'ragging', or the harassment of juniors by senior students. After introducing myself, I asked him, 'Are you happy?'

As soon he heard this question, his expression changed. His face lost all colour and tears began to roll down his eyes. *Oh no!* The psychologist in me wondered, panicked. *Did I ask the wrong question?* But something told me to wait. Sure enough, after a moment or two, he regained control of his

emotions and wiped away his tears. Rather than answer
my question directly, Ramsey began to reminisce about his
schooldays. He began by telling me how he had won the
Best Sportsman of the Year award for six consecutive years
in school. That obese boy, sportsman of the year? It was
unbelievable. He was in no shape to even walk properly!
What had happened to him?

Ignoring the look of astonishment on my face, he
continued telling me how he and his friend Joshua were
undefeatable when together. When they took to the crease
in a cricket match, they remained there till the end of the
game, taking their team to certain victory time and again.
They even represented their school at the national level.
Their friendship extended way beyond sports. Ramsey told
me that not even his parents understood him as well as
Joshua did. They were inseparable.

Then one day, things changed. Joshua's father got
transferred to a remote town very far from where they lived.
Before the two best friends could recover from the shock
or do something about it, within a week, the family had
moved out. With Joshua out of his life, Ramsey couldn't
identify with anyone else. No matter how hard he tried
to connect with people, no one made sense to him. His
interest in sports began to dwindle after he lost a couple of
important matches. In fact, he gave up cricket altogether.
His schoolmates, who earlier looked up to him, began to
ridicule him for his poor form. His grades nosedived. His
parents got worried and began to ask him what was wrong
but to no avail. He was desperate to find some solace and
that's when he discovered his love for food. Every time he

sank his teeth into tasty, mouth-watering dishes, he would forget all his worries. Soon, he became addicted to food.

It was when he told his own story aloud that it began to dawn on him—the connection between his love of food and his lost friendship. It was a 'eureka!' moment for him. He had never realized that he had subconsciously replaced a person he loved with food.

What happened to Ramsey happens to hundreds of young people around the world, though everyone does not turn to food the way he did. It is unfortunate that most people don't realize the impact losing friends can have on their habits. A particularly dangerous example of this was the case of Udisha. She and Tanya had been the best of buddies right from kindergarten. Over the years, their friendship blossomed beautifully, with fun, love and laughter all the way. When they became teenagers, their bond grew even stronger as together they discovered a whole new world within and without. But it was at this time, after secondary school, during the summer vacation, that they had their worst fight. They had had small fights in the past, like all friends do, but they eventually patched up in a day or two. But this time, their friendship suffered a major rift over Tanya's reluctance to share her study notes with Udisha. Both were toppers and though the friendship was intense, so was the competition. They stopped speaking to each other.

Two years passed and there was no communication. Finally, the silence was broken with the help of some other friends after their Board exams. As they spoke to each other, it seemed as if they were reconnecting with their lost selves. Having passed out from school, both were eager to catch up on old times. Udisha invited Tanya to her grandmother's place, of which they had great memories together. Udisha and Tanya used to go up to the roof of the old house, where no one bothered them, and spend hours talking about everything under the sun. Now, after two long years, they were at the same place again, having a heart-to-heart conversation. But in the middle of the chat, Tanya got the shock of her life. She saw Udisha light up a cigarette as they were talking. She looked at her friend closely, and noticed for the first time that her eyes seemed sunken and her lips dark and pale. Shocked and concerned, she asked her friend, 'Udisha, when did you start smoking, and why?'

There was no answer. Udisha responded with total silence.

Soon, Udisha started getting drowsy. An alarmed Tanya immediately snatched the half-burnt stick dangling between her fingers and threw it away.

Udisha screamed, 'Where were you all this while? It took you two years to do this? You left me and I started hanging out with a bunch of losers because no one else would be my friend. I've gotten addicted to all this stuff with them.'

Tanya's jaw dropped. 'What is it?' she asked.

'Heroin,' Udisha responded slowly, tears in her eyes. 'I can't do without it, Tanya . . .'

Tanya was shattered. She hugged her dear friend and they cried their hearts out as all the feelings that they'd been holding back for two years flowed free. Tanya too had spent the past two years pining for her friend. No one could truly replace Udisha. Their separation had made them miserable in many ways. They understood that it wasn't worth it all. They resumed their old friendship and also realized the responsibility they had towards each other. Soon, the happiness that they shared in their renewed friendship helped Udisha kick her drug habit.

Tanya and Udisha were lucky they got back together. People are often not able to do so and as they get older, it becomes more difficult.

C.S. Lewis once said, 'Friendship is born at that moment when one man says to another, "What! You too? I thought that no one but myself . . ."'

You've probably felt that way at some point in your life too. For life to feel complete, there should be at least one friend who evokes this feeling in your heart. This is a feeling of being in alignment with another human being, a feeling of being almost identical. Blood relationships are formed when you share DNA, the substance of the body. Friendship is formed when you share the substance of the mind.

Most people today form friendships due to circumstances. These are called 'circumstantial friendships'. Though some of them may end up becoming genuinely deep bonds, usually, they do not cross the first level of friendship. Now you may think, 'What is Level 1 of friendship? How many levels does friendship have?' Let me introduce you to the various levels of friendship before we take this conversation ahead. I will start with an example.

Kamla was a smart and talented girl. It was no wonder she was popular in college. She also knew what made people happy: a little bit of kindness and a few words of appreciation. She used these generously in her dealings with everyone, and people were drawn towards her. Her life was busy, what with so many invitations and so many friends wanting her company all the time. She was always surrounded by people. Life felt like it could not have been better or happier for Kamla.

One day, she woke very excited: they were celebrating Friendship Day in college. She had given a lot of thought to the matter of whom she wanted to give gifts to. She had many friends to choose from and she didn't want anyone to feel left out. But she couldn't possibly give gifts to each and every friend she had! So she finally settled on two people she had recently befriended. Of course, she was as excited about receiving gifts as she was about giving them. However, she was not prepared for what happened next.

She sought out both her friends, as she had planned, and gave them their gifts. They laughed and smiled as they chatted, but they did not give anything to her. She waited all day for gifts to come her way. She had imagined friends falling all over her, showering gifts on her. But nothing like that happened. In fact, she was the only girl in class who did not receive a single gift! She was in such shock that she went home in tears. How was it that a girl who was the life of every party did not receive a single present? Did she not smile and hug her friends often enough? Did she not call them regularly to chat with them? Did she not attend their parties when they invited her? All this and yet, no one thought of her as a friend? It was too much for her to bear.

Her family consoled her, but her mother pointed out that perhaps, in her effort to be a friend to everyone, she had not been a true friend to anyone; in an attempt to win a large number of friends, she had undermined the importance of building quality friendships. Kamla understood her mother's words, but what could she do now?

She sought advice from her elder brother, who was her complete opposite in many ways. He said, 'Kamla, you cannot make friends just by using nice or kind words. True friends give each other time. They stay together through thick and thin.'

It did not make sense to Kamla. 'If I give my time to only a few people, what about others? I want to have lots of friends.'

Her brother explained, 'You can't have many close friends. There's only so much time you have. But some can be acquaintances, some can be closer and some can be your truly close friends. As you go up the pyramid, the number of your friends decreases but your bonding and closeness increase.'

That was the day that Kamla truly understood the different levels of friendship.

Here's how it works: broadly speaking, based on my understanding, there are four levels of friendship.

Four Levels of Friendship

Level 1: Bandhus or Associates

I can assure you that 95 per cent of your friendships will not grow beyond this level. These are relationships with people who just happen to be around us—neighbours, schoolmates, college-mates, colleagues, etc. They are not all necessarily our friends, but are *bandhus* or associates. Yes, someone who is a bandhu or an associate can eventually become a Level-4 friend, but every associate need not be a friend. Using various levels to describe friendships is an easy way to understand the different kinds of interpersonal connections.

Having associates is very important. In fact, the more associates you have, the better it is. These are people you will find around yourself everywhere. Being acquainted with your neighbours is always helpful. The more you engage with your colleagues, the more your knowledge bank will grow. Not everyone knows everything, but everyone knows something.

When I was in school, many of my schoolmates and I would get together and divide the various topics of a subject between us. Each of us would thoroughly study and understand the topic allotted to him. Then we would come together and explain our topics to each other. Thus, collectively, we would end up studying much faster and better than we could have individually. It is just that this didn't make us friends as much as it made us bandhus or associates collaborating on a project.

To put it in a nutshell, associates share experiences and learning. They often come together for a purpose and when that purpose is met, they part. One should reach out to these associates as often as one can.

Once, a college professor created a unique exercise for his students to drive home the importance of friendliness at work and in the neighbourhood. He tied chopsticks to the elbows of a few students so that they could not bend their arms. Then he sat them down at a table with noodles in front of them, instructing them to eat. It was a funny sight to see them try. They all dropped their noodles as their arms would not bend. How on earth would they eat? Maybe the professor was testing their patience. At first, everyone attempted to eat without a thought for how the others were faring. After many futile attempts, everyone looked at the others. None of them had managed to eat. They sat and wondered some more. Then one of them had a brainwave. He twirled the noodles around his chopsticks and offered to feed his neighbour. The neighbour was only too happy to finally be able to meet. The neighbour fed his neighbour, and then his neighbour fed his neighbour, and so on. In no time, they all polished off the noodles and sat smiling with delight at their achievement.

The professor had been watching them keenly and at the end of the exercise, congratulated them. They had learnt the art of helping each other and collaborating successfully by simply being friendly with each another.

It is a verified fact that collaboration between a team's members makes the team more effective. Working with associates not only brings joy but may also produce better results than working with people you don't know well enough to seek help from or provide help to.

Level 2: Sakhas or Friends

There will be some people in your life who are not content being bandhus. They will enter the second level of friendship with you. They are called *sakhas* or friends. These are people who have managed to make inroads into your heart. These inroads are cemented by a very powerful building material: time.

These are people who do not want to compete with you; instead, they look for ways to complement you. Sakhas encourage you and push you way more than you can push yourself. They can see the good in you even when you can't see it in yourself. The more they know about you, the more they can help you. The more they understand your forte, the more they will help to push you towards your goal. They help you so much that you might wonder what they get out of it. Well, the answer is satisfaction! Sakhas thrive on the satisfaction they derive from helping you grow and achieve your full potential. They are interested in your success because they are interested in their satisfaction. The more you grow, the more satisfied they are.

Sakhas don't envy your growth because they know that in your growth lies theirs. They act as bridges that help you connect with others. Since such people thrive on other people's growth, they usually have large social circles and know many people. Because they have invested in others' growth, they have actually invested in the expansion of their networks. Their strength lies in the connections they form with others. Their fuel is other people's gratitude. They feel great about themselves when others express their gratefulness to them.

Often, we take our sakhas for granted. We assume that they will always be there for us when we reach out to them and thus forget to express gratitude and appreciation, but it is important to remember that it is an expression of gratitude and genuine appreciation that builds deeper friendships. It is not easy to find a good sakha or friend; they are usually among a small percentage of the people remaining on your friends' list after you filter out the associates. When you do find such wonderful souls, latch on to them. They are your primary sources of growth and networking.

Level 3: Priya Sakhas or Confidential Friends

These are an even rarer species of friends. They are people you love to be with. Every time you enjoy their company, you come back supercharged and happy. While bandhus and sakhas might make you happy most of the time, they might still let you down sometimes. But *priya sakhas* never let you down. In fact, they know how to pick you up when you are down. They know exactly what to say to make you happy. They know how to make you smile all the time. They usually have great stories that lift your spirits. They avoid all negative talk and negative thoughts. They may even crack stupid jokes in their attempt to keep the environment around you positive. The more you are in touch with their positive energy, the happier you will be.

Priya sakhas make you better versions of yourself. They challenge you, they shake you awake from your slumber and they shape you by logically compelling you to upgrade your thoughts and actions. With them around you, you can never remain the old version of yourself for too long. They constantly push you towards positive changes in life. In every situation, priya sakhas will help you see things from a totally different perspective that you might never have if not for them.

The problem with being with such people is that it's not easy to be with them, but then, improvement is never easy. Though they are fun to be with, when it comes to the question of your growth, they usually act tough. At such times, it is important that you don't push your priya sakhas away. Even if you don't understand their ideas right away, give them some time to sink in. Don't react immediately. Learn to honour their viewpoints, even if you do not agree with them. They usually think of your betterment at least a few years before you do. Learn to converse with them with an unbiased outlook. They are not called trusted friends for no reason. They can expand the horizons of your thinking and your life beyond your comprehension. Cherish them, for they are hard to find and nearly impossible to replace.

Level 4: Suhrits or Best Friends

Usually, this type of friend is one in a million. They make up 0.01 per cent of your friends' list: the rarest of rare bonds. A *suhrit* is always there for you no matter what phase of life you are in. When anything major happens to you in life, suhrits tend to be the first people you turn to. The friendship is so deep that many times, words are not necessary for you to understand each other's feelings. There is such alignment and understanding that even before you say it, they know it. A suhrit doesn't live for himself or herself, they live for their friend. There is an element of sacrifice involved in this level of friendship. Your suhrit is likely to stand up for you even if no one in the world does and will do so even in your absence; they hold your hand and help you overcome your fears. They don't judge you; they accept you as you are. When you succeed, they are proud of you and when you fail, they cry with you. They help you stand when you fall and grow when you stand; they do all this simply because they love you unconditionally.

When one discusses one's success with others, there is usually the fear of being considered too proud and when one tries to discuss one's failures with others, there is the fear of being considered weak. However, suhrits are people with whom you can share both your successes and failures without the fear of being judged. You can share your weaknesses and mistakes with them without the fear of being criticized. You can confide in them and trust them to keep it confidential. With suhrits, you don't have to waste time talking about petty stuff. Instead, you talk about the key events in your life that shape you, and they help you navigate the journey of life expertly. They not only show you the right direction, but walk with you till you reach your destination. Conversations with a suhrit are usually at such a level that other people sometimes may not even understand what the two of you are talking about.

However, it is important that when you do find a suhrit, you try to be a suhrit to that person in return. Don't just dump your problems and worries on him or her. Instead, try to spend some time looking silently at their world with interest and keep a keen ear. The more you share, the more you bond. Being there for one another mutually strengthens both of you. A suhrit often finds reasons to respect you even more than you respect yourself, which is why they deserve to be respected in return and be trusted totally. Don't let them down. Because what they give is more than what you can ever expect from them.

Let us take the example of two friends, Sid and Jimmy. Sid had fractured his hand in a car accident and now that it had healed, he was waiting for the nurse to remove the cast. He seemed impatient and urged the nurse to hurry up. The nurse asked him gently why he was so anxious. 'Your fracture has healed, no need to worry,' she said, trying to placate him.

Sid said, 'I have another appointment to rush to.'

'Where are you going that is so important?' the nurse inquired.

With his eyes tearing up, Sid replied, 'In the same car accident, my friend Jimmy injured his head and lost his memory. The doctor feels that if I talk to him every day about our life before the accident, he may be able to recover more quickly. So every day without fail, before going to office, I go and meet him. I talk about a lot of things, but he does not remember anything. Not even me.'

The nurse was surprised. 'If he does not recognize you, why do you go?'

Sid said softly, 'Because I still recognize him.'

In this story, Sid is a fine example of a suhrit. If you have found a suhrit, you have found a friendship that will last a lifetime. This is the highest level of friendship that humans can ever experience; it is a bond that is concrete and complete.

Okay, now that you know the different kinds of friends you have, let us move on to another important aspect of the phenomenon of friendship. I am going to tell you a fable that you have probably heard from your grandmother or read in primary school textbooks many years ago. But this popular fable is still relevant to understanding friendship. This is from the *Panchatantra*, the book of tales that educates us about various aspects of life. So far, we have read about how friendship is important to our lives and about the four kinds of friends most people make. Through this story, we learn about the first aspect of friendship: how we should choose our friends.

Raktamukha was a red-faced monkey who lived on a huge tree laden with the most succulent *jambu* fruits. He didn't have to take a single step in any direction because all his needs were fulfilled by the tree; he was a happy monkey with a happy home. The jambu tree was on the banks of a huge river. One day, while Raktamukha was busy feasting on his favourite fruits, he heard a strange sound coming from beneath the tree. Peering down from his perch, the monkey saw a huge crocodile resting its tired limbs on the soft sand below the branches and enjoying the shade of the tree.

Raktamukha, happy at having a guest visit him, immediately welcomed the crocodile, who introduced himself as Karalamukha. Asking him to open his mouth wide, the monkey dropped in a bunch of tasty jambu fruits. When Karalamukha took his first bite, his eyes widened and a big smile lit up his face. He had never eaten anything as tasty as that in his life! This was magical. When the crocodile appreciated the fruits, the monkey was thrilled and stuffed dozens more jambu fruits into the mouth of the crocodile, who ate them with great relish. When they were full, the two of them got talking about various things. Soon, they struck up a close friendship. They talked as comfortably as if they had known each other for ages. They loved each other's company. Hours passed in this happy conversation, but it seemed like only minutes. Finally, the crocodile departed for his home, only to return the next day. His love for the jambu fruits and for his newfound friend only increased by the day.

Karalamukha began to carry back with him a bunch of fruits for his wife. She loved them too. One day, the clever wife told her husband that the heart of the monkey that eats such tasty fruits must be even tastier! She began to insist that her husband get her the monkey's heart. Karalamukha was shocked at his wife's demand. How could he do that to his friend? That too to a friend who had fed him so much and with whom he had shared such lovely memories? The wife became even more adamant at seeing his reluctance. Left with no choice, the morose crocodile swam towards his friend's abode with a plan in mind.

As usual, Raktamukha was overjoyed seeing his friend approach his tree. He had collected a huge bunch of the choicest fruits for his friend that day. Sitting next to his friend, he began to offer them to him. Karalamukha seemed distant that day and did not respond in his usual warm manner. Finally, he told the monkey that his wife was extremely upset with him. He explained that the cause of her anger was his ungrateful attitude. For many days he had been eating the food his friend provided, but never did he gratefully reciprocate the kindness. He said that his wife wanted him to bring his friend along for a meal to their beautiful island house as a gesture of gratitude.

The monkey was happy with the invitation. He said, 'Your wife is absolutely right. A person shouldn't be like a weaver who always pulls the cloth towards himself. One shouldn't always keep receiving but should also learn to give. I would have been happy to come but the problem is that I am a forest dweller and your home is in the middle of an island. How will I swim across deep waters? It would be best if your wife came here and we dined together.'

The crocodile panicked at the possibility of his plan being derailed and was extremely fearful of having to face the wrath of his wife. He tried desperately to think of a way out. He suddenly had a brainwave. 'You may not be able to swim, but remember, you have a friend who can swim extremely well. You have to simply climb onto my back and in a matter of minutes, we will be home, relishing the delicacies prepared by my wife, who is an expert cook,' said Karalamukha.

Left with no choice, the monkey agreed, and the two friends began the river cruise with the monkey seated on the crocodile's back and the crocodile gliding across the river smoothly. The monkey had never ventured so far into the waters. Swimming close to the shore was one thing, but being in the middle of that massive river was a totally different experience. There was no way the monkey could go back or even go anywhere else from here. The crocodile was acutely aware that he was letting his friend down. The guilt was eating him up. But there was not much he could do about it due to the adamancy of his wife. The least he could do was to prepare his friend to face the inevitable.

With a heavy heart, he finally spoke. 'My friend, I want to tell you something that you must know at this point. My wife has developed a desire to eat your heart. She thinks that your heart will be the tastiest monkey heart in the world because it's been relishing so much of the nectar of the jambu fruits. Though I do not wish to harm you, I have to fulfil my wife's desire.'

The monkey was shocked by the sudden revelation and the unforeseen turn of events. He knew that there was no way to escape from the clutches of the crocodile in the middle of the river. His mind began racing, looking for an escape plan. Suddenly, he hit upon an idea. He said, 'O friend! Why didn't you tell me before? Had I known of this desire of your wife, I would have got my heart along. I have this habit of leaving my precious heart on the tree for safety when I go on outings.'

Karalamukha was a foolish crocodile and immediately broke into a sweat in the middle of the river. He could almost see the anger in his wife's eyes. He would be dead if she discovered that he had got the monkey without his heart! He began to panic. He couldn't swim any farther and came to a standstill. Raktamukha smiled seeing his plan work. Now was the time to implement the next part of the plan.

He spoke reassuringly to his so-called friend, 'Don't worry, friend. I won't let you down. Let's just go back home and get my heart. It may delay your wife's meal but at least she will get to relish what she wants.'

That made sense to the dim-witted crocodile. He turned around and swam back towards the monkey's tree house. As soon as the crocodile got close enough, the monkey made a run for his life. In a jiffy, he reached the highest branch of the tree and held on to it tightly for dear life. The crocodile was confused. Why wasn't he coming down with his heart? He looked up and called out to his friend. He told him that they had to get home soon, else his wife would be angry. The monkey smiled and quoted a Sanskrit verse:

Dadati pratighrinati
ghuyam akhayati prichhati
bhunkte bhojayate chaiva
shad vidha priti lakshanam

(Giving and receiving gifts, revealing one's heart in confidence and listening to another's confidential revelation, inviting to dine and being invited to dine. These are the six loving exchanges that enhance friendships.)

'But these six loving exchanges should be performed between people who are like-minded. You are a crocodile and I am a monkey. Though there are some things common between us that created a loving bond, we can never be friends at a higher level because of the differences between us. Now that I know how cruel your mind is and how little you value our friendship, I cannot give my heart to you. When I told you that I left my heart on the tree,

I wasn't referring to the physical heart. You are so foolish that you think that the physical heart can be removed and kept aside. I was talking about giving my heart to you in friendship. The moment you told me your cruel intentions, I realized that you don't deserve my friendship. I made a mistake thinking that someone who lives in the middle of a river could be a true friend to me.'

The crocodile realized that he had been fooled. Not only that, he also realized that he had lost a good friend and that he may never eat the sweet jambu fruit again!

The Joy of Having Like-Minded Friends

The most important element of friendship is like-mindedness. When people of similar dispositions connect with one another, the bond that is formed does not snap under any sort of pressure or circumstance. This does not mean that people who are of different mindsets cannot be friends. The key is in the depth of their connection. A Persian poet put it beautifully, 'I saw a grass bush surround a rose plant. In great anger, I cried, "How dare the lowly grass live in the proximity of the majestic roses?" But just as I was about to pluck the grass, its feeble voice spoke up in all humility: "Please allow me to stay. I may not be a rose, but my fragrance will tell anyone that I have at least lived with the great roses."' The question we should ask here is 'how long can grass and roses stay together?' Sure, they can benefit from each other for some time, but to live together, they need more than just proximity.

How does one make like-minded friends? Jim Rohn was an American entrepreneur, author and motivational speaker. He believed that one becomes an average of five people one is with most. Most people become friends because of circumstances. Studying in the same school, studying in the same university, working in the same company, staying in the same neighbourhood, exercising in the same gym, playing in the same club: all these lead to circumstantial friendships. Circumstances shouldn't be the basis of friendship. Many people choose their friends based on material well-being—wealth, popularity, power, cars, cool gadgets, entry into the best parties; all this and more can become the cause of friendship sometimes. However, such friendship is selfish and transient.

Friendships are crucial to the well-being of every individual. But they cannot be developed overnight. They need patient nursing, which requires time. Loving bonds grow in three stages. The first stage is like a nursery; the second stage is like a garden and the third stage is like a forest. The nursery stage of any relationship is the stage in which the saplings of love are growing. They are very young and need to be protected from many external sources of tension and internal misunderstandings. If there is inadequate care and precaution at this stage, the sapling of love will never grow into a full-fledged plant. When love between friends develops further, it reaches the garden stage. There are small saplings in the nursery, but in a garden, they all transform into mature plants. This is how friendship also grows, from Level 1 to Level 3, over time.

But there are some very special friendships that grow even beyond that. They reach the fourth stage of love, which is the forest stage. A forest is so big that one need not plant anything—in every direction, there are innumerable trees. This is the stage of love that constitutes a Level-4 friendship. A lot of care has to be taken in cultivating a nursery and a garden. But once love takes the shape of a forest, you don't need to give it constant care—there are no real threats that can harm the bond. This is Level-4 friendship. One in a million friends will reach this stage of friendship with anyone; it would be ideal if everyone had at least one friend like that.

Did I become too serious? Let's lighten up. Let me tell you a story about a friendship from the Indian epics. The Mahabharata talks about a Level-4 friendship. This is probably the best example of a suhrit or best friend I have found. Remember, there is an element of sacrifice involved in such friendships, which is relatively rare these days. If you have one suhrit in your life, you will be the happiest person alive. And if you become a suhrit to someone, you will be the most cherished person.

'He who removes fear from your mind is the greatest friend.' This translation of the proverb in Sanskrit best describes the legendary connection between Arjuna and Krishna—the depth of their friendship was unbelievable. They stood by each other during good and bad times alike. Even when their own family members misunderstood them, they didn't misunderstand each other. The greatest test of their friendship was in a decisive moment that would change the world. Just before the war of Kurukshetra, both Duryodhana and Arjuna came to Krishna for help. Krishna gave them a choice: either the Narayana sena of Dwarka, an undefeatable, fully equipped military force, or Krishna himself, unarmed and unwilling to fight in the war. He asked Arjuna to choose first as he wanted to test his friendship. Was Arjuna interested in his friendship or in the perks of his friendship? Was he interested in him or in what he could gain through him? As is obvious, he chose Krishna—he chose friendship over the perks of friendship. For him, having his best friend by his side meant having the whole world on his side.

When anything major happened in Arjuna's life, he would first turn to his suhrit, Krishna. Their friendship was so deep that words didn't have to be spoken for them to understand each other's feelings. There was so much alignment and understanding that even before Arjuna could say it, Krishna would know it. Krishna never lived for himself, he lived for his friends. They were friends who could literally die for each other. Their friendship would last beyond a lifetime. It was a bond that was both concrete and complete. Krishna would stand up for Arjuna even if no one else in the world did, even if Arjuna was not aware of his support. He was always there to alleviate Arjuna's fears and anxieties. He didn't judge Arjuna, he accepted him as he was. When Arjuna succeeded, Krishna was very proud of him and when he failed, Krishna cried with him. Krishna did all this simply because he loved Arjuna unconditionally.

Arjuna narrated both his successes and his failures to Krishna without the fear of being judged. He shared his weaknesses and mistakes with Krishna without the fear of being criticized. He could confide in Krishna and trust him to keep his secrets. Krishna helped Arjuna navigate his life expertly. Arjuna's conversations with his suhrit, Krishna, compiled into the Bhagavadgita, are so timeless and profound that even today, people are unpacking the wisdom in what they were talking about. In confusion, Krishna became a guide to Arjuna. In war, he became a strategist. In times of difficulty, he became a source of hope. In good times, Krishna became a wonderful companion for Arjuna. In poverty, Krishna became a catalyst for the growth that would allow Arjuna to change his circumstances. A suhrit takes on the role their best friend needs them to play at the time. In addition to everything they did for one another, Krishna and Arjuna also respected each other greatly. A suhrit is someone who respects you more than you respect yourself. Each time Krishna called out to Arjuna, he called him by a different name, which signified a particular good quality in Arjuna that he was appreciating. Arjuna reciprocated in the same way.

Wow! Wasn't that something? Don't you wish you could have even one such suhrit in your life? We can't choose our relatives but thank God, we can choose our friends. You should always be careful about your choice of friends. As the famous Spanish author Miguel de Cervantes has said, 'Tell me thy company, and I'll tell thee what thou art.' The friends we choose define us. Just like companies conduct a yearly audit to evaluate every aspect of the organization, it's a good idea to conduct a 'friendship audit' every now and then to find out how your friendships are faring, which friendships are worth investing in, which ones are bringing you down and thus need to be avoided. Try finding like-mindedness with your friends—see with whom you experience the greatest like-mindedness and with whom you experience the least.

There is probably no better way of describing good friendships than sage Bhartrihari's words from a verse in the *Neeti Shatakam*. This Sanskrit verse uses an analogy that is so commonly seen but rarely thought about.

Kshireshaatma gatodakaaya
hi ghusha dattam puraa te'khila
kshirottaapam avekshya tena
pasyam svaatmam krus'aanau hutah
gantuh paavakam unmanas
tad abhavad drushtvaa tu mitraapadh
yukta teena jalena smayati
sataha maîtri punastvidrusii

(One can learn all about friendship from the relationship between milk and water. They love each other so much that when water is added to milk, milk lends its good qualities to water and water adds to the quantity of milk. When water finds that milk is in danger of boiling over, it first sacrifices itself by jumping into the fire to save its friend. When milk finds that its friend is in such a dangerous situation, it also jumps into the fire, unable to bear the separation from its friend. When they both live together in normal conditions, they are happy and peaceful because they love each other so much and are so like-minded that they share their worlds.)

We should look for these three qualities, which characterize the friendship of milk and water, if we want to form lasting friendships:

1. The ability to complement one another.
2. The ability to sacrifice for one another.
3. Like-mindedness. Just like milk and water complement each other, genuine friends also complement each other and help one another overcome their shortcomings.

It is important to remember that neither is complete or perfect, but when they come together, they help each other. Without an element of sacrifice, friendships remain superficial. One sacrifices only for those who are dear to the heart. No one sacrifices for the sake of strangers. It is also much easier to sacrifice for those who play an important role in our lives. The moment one performs any kind of sacrifice for one's friend, one actually strengthens one's hold on the heart of that friend.

Sacrifice unites while selfishness divides. For two people to bond, there has to be a feeling of oneness. That oneness is about cultural, social, spiritual, emotional and intellectual like-mindedness. It is not possible for two people to be like-minded about everything in life. But for friendship to last, there has to be like-mindedness at least about the most important aspects of life, those which matter to both.

Summary:

- We saw how important friendship is; how crucial it can be for survival itself.
- We saw, through examples, how cracks in friendship can lead to self-damaging choices like overeating, addiction and depression.
- We also saw positive examples like the deep friendship between Arjuna and Krishna, who were each other's life and soul, so much so that Arjuna had earned the nickname Krishna.

Activity

This is your Wheel of Friendship that will help analyze all your friendships.

You are at the centre of the wheel. As you move outwards, the depth of your relationship starts becoming shallow. The outermost circle represents friends who are bandhu or level-1. Take some time to identify upto ten relationships that fall in the bandhu category. As you move towards the centre from Level 1, the next circle represents sakhas or level 2. Choose upto six relationships that qualify as sakhas. You may even want to shift some from the bandhus to the sakha category. The next inner circle represents priya sakhas or level 3. Who are your priya sakhas? Write down their names. The closest circle to you are your suhrits or level-4 friends. Is there anyone who fits the bill? Yes, that's great. No? Then underline a few names you would like to have as suhrits. Are you a suhrit for them? This wheel now gives you a graphic analysis of who stands at which level in your world.

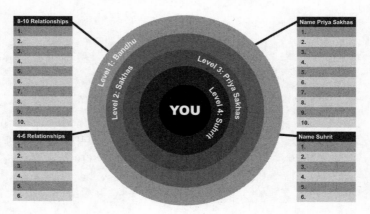

8-10 Relationships
1.
2.
3.
4.
5.
6.
7.
8.
9.
10.

4-6 Relationships
1.
2.
3.
4.
5.
6.

Level 1: Bandhu
Level 2: Sakhas
Level 3: Priya Sakhas
Level 4: Suhrit
YOU

Name Priya Sakhas
1.
2.
3.
4.
5.
6.
7.
8.
9.
10.

Name Suhrit
1.
2.
3.
4.
5.
6.

2

How Good a Friend Are You?

Yes, that would be my first question—how good a friend are you? Because to have a strong friendship, you need to be a good friend. Sometimes, a little positive change in your behaviour can bring about positive changes in the nature of your friendship.

Let's take this further: ask yourself a few questions. Are you adequately prepared to be a good friend to someone? Do you have what it takes to be a friend? We prepare for everything important in life, don't we? We prepare for admissions into the best of universities, we prepare for exams, we prepare for debates, for job interviews, for appraisals and for performance reviews. But why is it that we feel that we either do not need to prepare, or that we are already prepared, to enter into a friendship?

To help you understand this, let me start by telling you a Greek legend. When man was first created, Zeus, the father of the Greek gods, gave him two bags. The first bag contained the man's own faults and the second bag

31

contained the faults of everyone else. In order to help him carry both bags, Zeus also gave him a long stick, on the two ends of which he could hang the two bags and balance them. Unfortunately, while handing man the stick, Zeus made a grave mistake due to which man suffers to this day.

Want to know what that big mistake was?

Zeus handed the stick such that the bag containing the faults of others was hung in front of him and the bag containing man's own faults was hung behind him. It is said that as a result of this, man was easily able to see other people's faults, but could rarely ever see his own. That is why the ability to find faults in everyone except oneself is called 'the Zeus fault'. We are all struggling rather desperately with the Zeus fault. If we want to prepare for friendship, we have to first learn to spot our own shortcomings and then rectify them. Before you beat others, you need to achieve victory over yourself. As Jon Maxwell says in his book *25 Ways To Win With People*, your relationships can be only as healthy as you are.

Now let me tell you about two other gifts that we were given as soon as we were created: a mirror and a lens. These are not used for the first few years of our lives, when we are still babies. But as soon as we become a little older, we begin to use them. The mirror helps us see ourselves and the lens enables us to see others. Using the mirror, we become aware of our weaknesses and shortcomings—it helps us identify, accept and then address our incompleteness. The lens makes us aware of our short-sightedness and overlook others' shortcomings. Because of the Zeus fault, it is easy for us to find faults in others. Just like Sunita ended up doing—finding faults with her neighbour. Let me tell you her story.

Sunita moved into a new neighbourhood with her husband Nikhil. She instantly fell in love with their new house. It was one in a series of row houses neatly built in perfect alignment with one another. Once they settled down, they got into their daily routine. One day, as they were seated at the dining table eating their breakfast, Sunita commented, 'Look at our neighbour's laundry. Does it look like they've washed their clothes? They are so dirty even after being washed. I wonder who taught her to wash like that.'

Nikhil looked in the direction Sunita had indicated, smiled and turned again to his plate, while Sunita continued staring at her neighbour's shabby clothes. The next day, Sunita again brought up the subject of the neighbour's dirty linen at the breakfast table. It seemed to bother her very much. She was considering walking up to the neighbour and suggesting either a change of detergent or learning to wash clothes the right way, but she somehow managed to restrain herself and tried not to look in that direction the whole day. The next morning, when she happened to look out of the window, she was in for a pleasant surprise. Hanging on the clothes line was a set of brilliantly white, shining, spotlessly clean clothes. Sunita actually stood up in surprise. 'How is it that the clothes are so clean today?' she asked aloud. It was then that Nikhil smiled and told her casually that he had cleaned their windows the previous night. Sunita was astounded by the revelation but embarrassed too, realizing that the dirt she kept seeing was not on the neighbour's clean laundry but actually on her own window.

Sunita's window represents the Zeus fault, but it also helps understand the purpose of the lens. Just like Sunita looked through her window, we look through our lens, eager to find fault in others. But as we focus on other's faults, we seldom realize that the fault might actually be our own! With an unclean lens, we cannot expect to see a clean image of others. Hence, before we look through our lens, we need to clean the lens. And to clean the lens, we have to look into the mirror. The mirror will help us see our own faults, become aware of the Zeus fault in us and finally notice the bag of our own faults hanging behind us, hidden from our view.

In India, when people get angry at each other, a phrase they often use is, 'Go look at yourself in the mirror!' which is supposed to mean that you should first go and look at your own faults before blaming or judging others for their actions.

What many of us don't understand is that there are two ways of looking into the mirror. One way is the superficial way. The second way of looking into the mirror is the deeper, more introspective way. Now, I know hundreds of youngsters who spend hours in front of the mirror every single day. They seem to have fallen in love with whom they see there. However, if you look at yourself in the second way, the more deeply you look at your image in the mirror, the more clearly the mirror reveals your realities to you. You will come closer to an awareness of your image. Most of us are so unaware of our reality that we don't have any realization of it.

When simply understanding yourself is so complex, how do you go about correcting yourself? No matter how wisely others advise you on improving yourself, no matter how many books you read on self-improvement, no matter how many inspiring videos you watch on self-development, the onus of bringing about a change in yourself rests solely on you. No one in the world can help you unless you help yourself. This *subhashitam* or verse of wisdom aptly explains what I am trying to say:

Swabhavo nopadeshena
Shakyate krtumanyatha
Sutaptamapi paaniyam
Punargacchati shitataam

(No amount of good advice can change the nature of a person. Just like water, when heated, returns to its original temperature in some time, even if a person changes his behaviour when advised by others, he will soon return to his intrinsic nature)

No one else can help us change our nature. We should have the desire to work on it ourselves. Others can assist to some extent, but the responsibility to create change is ours. Most people in this world are like water; when you 'heat' or excite them by giving them a pep talk or a session of counselling, you immediately find some changes in them; suddenly, they seem to transform. But once the memory of that advice or stimulation wears off, they are back to square one. Why do you think people are hooked to motivational videos on social media nowadays? It is because they get an artificial feeling of something changing in themselves. Unfortunately, the inspiration is short-lived and so is the change!

There is a critical difference between what we see on social media that brings no change and what can actually bring about a change. What people mean when they talk about change today is called 'behavioural change'. Behavioural change is easy, but changing one's consciousness is difficult. Behavioural change is reversible, but change in consciousness is irreversible. Behavioural change is short-lived, but change in consciousness is eternal. Looking into the mirror superficially leads to behavioural change. Looking into the mirror deeply and introspectively is what leads to change at the level of one's consciousness.

This gazing into oneself is the first step in readying oneself for friendship.

Gazing into the mirror at yourself is like observing your state of mind. A self-absorbed or selfish person sees everything and everyone from their point of view and from their frame of reference alone. Everything we see and focus on reflects the state of our mind. Everything we see in others reflects the state of our mind. Everything we see in life situations reflects the state of our mind. Therefore, it is critical to first examine the state of one's mind. Let me tell you another story from the Mahabharata to explain this crucial point better: Guru Dronacharya had the most talented disciples any teacher could aspire to have. It was a pleasure to teach them and also a joy to see them absorb everything so enthusiastically and efficiently. He not only gave them knowledge and skills, but also focused on their character development. Ever so often, he would test his disciples in unusual ways. These tests, though seemingly innocent, were psychological tests that gave him an insight into their minds. Drona loved to study his disciples' mindsets so that he could mould them to be better leaders and, more importantly, better people.

One day, he called Duryodhana, one of the most vocal and aggressive of his disciples, and gave him an unusual task. Drona told him to go out into the city and find someone who was better than him. Duryodhana thought a lot about it and devised a set of questions to ask people that would help him compare their strengths, skills and talents with his. But he didn't have to ask most people even one question. Just by looking at them, he could scan their defects and shortcomings immediately. By the end of the day, he had become quite an expert at finding fault with people and had completely stopped asking questions. Finally, his project was complete. He walked up to his teacher with his findings. His answer was simple: there was absolutely no one in the kingdom who was better than him. In every person, he had found some defect that he didn't have. He had, in fact, maintained a detailed 'database' of every person he had met and a list of the defects he had found in them.

Drona was impressed by Duryodhana's ability to find defects in everyone in the kingdom in such a short period of time. However, not saying a word, Drona kept looking towards the gate. He was waiting for someone to return. And then there he was, Yudhishthira, another disciple, returning after having completed another test. Though the tasks were similar, the questions were subtly different. He had instructed Yudhishthira to go around the city and find at least one person who was worse than him. Like Duryodhana, Yudhishthira, too, had travelled the length and breadth of the kingdom interviewing and observing people. He, too, had come back with a negative answer. He couldn't find even one person in the entire land who was worse than him. He found at least one good quality in each person which he didn't possess. In fact, he was ashamed that there were so many good qualities that he was nowhere close to cultivating in himself. He was determined to work on himself. Drona smiled at his findings.

He called both his disciples. He told Duryodhana that he had just found one person who was better than him—it was Yudhishthira. He then turned to Yudhishthira and told him that he had just found one person who was worse than him—and that was Duryodhana.

Through this test, Drona taught us all a very important lesson. Someone who is not able to find fault in himself is filled with faults, and someone who is not able to find fault in others has risen above the greatest human fault, which is fault-finding. While Duryodhana viewed everyone in the land through Sunita's dirty window and a lens clouded by the Zeus fault, Yudhishthira chose to spend that time viewing himself introspectively through the mirror. The more fault he found with himself, the more good he could find in others. The more he mused on his own shortcomings, the more he could appreciate greatness in others and look beyond their defects. Duryodhana's lens and Yudhishthira's mirror are the two different ways we look at the world. Most of us prefer Duryodhana's lens because it seems like the easiest thing to do and doesn't make you uncomfortable. It is much harder to examine yourself before you perceive the world, as Yudhishthira did. Everything and everyone we see reflects the state of our own mind. Duryodhana's mind was inclined only to seeing fault in others because he was trying to prove that he was faultless and perfect. Yudhishthira's mind was inclined only to seeing goodness in others because he had learnt to first value the goodness in himself and was therefore able to see it in others. In an ocean of goodness, Duryodhana was an expert at finding fault. In an ocean of shortcomings, Yudhishthira was an expert in finding the gems of good qualities.

The only question we have to ask ourselves to become aware of our own worldview is, 'Do I have the honesty to admit that I have defects that I need to overcome?' Because if you don't look, you won't find. If you don't find, how will you admit your faults? If you won't admit them, how will you work on them? If you don't work on them, how will you prepare yourself for others? And if you are not your own friend, how can you be a friend to another person? To be a friend to another person, you first need to be a friend to yourself. Before you take on the responsibility of a friendship, you first need to take responsibility for your own self. The responsibility for changing 'me' does not lie with others. It is solely your own responsibility.

Have you ever noticed how difficult it is to change? There is something within us that doesn't allow us to change, and it is this very thing that controls our vision and perception of others and of the world around us. It even affects the way we deal with major life events. Let me tell you about a very funny animation film that I watched in my childhood, which illustrates this very point very well. Though I don't remember all the details of this particular film, there is one small episode that is still stuck in my head. I am reminded of it every now and then. In this episode, there was a honeybee that loved to drink honey from flowers. One day, as was his routine, he left the honeycomb early in the morning, when he was still sleepy. But it was time for work and everyone was pushed out to go and collect honey for the day. Since it was his routine, he knew the way by heart and could reach the garden with his eyes closed. That's exactly what he did that day in trying to catch a few more winks while hovering towards his destination, the garden. But unfortunately, there was some obstacle in his way that day and before he realized that it was there, he had banged against something hard and fallen into flowing sewage. Luckily, his reflexes were good so he got out, but he still ended up getting all mucky. Shrugging off all the dirt, the bee flew towards his haven; he needed to smell something better to forget the awful stink of the sewage. The bee longed to sit on the beautiful flowers, soaking in the heavenly fragrance and devouring the sweet, ambrosial honey. Hovering over the many flowers, he finally settled down on the most beautiful one. But horror of horrors! He was aghast to find that no matter how hard he tried to inhale the fragrance of the flower, he could only smell the stink of sewage. Could it be that this particular flower was contaminated with the water from the sewage? He went to another flower and the same smell pervaded that one as well. He went to yet another and the same foul odour followed him. Every single flower in the garden smelled simply awful! Seeing his confused state, another bee came to his rescue and revealed to him that the dirty smell was not coming from the flowers but from the dirt that was stuck to his antennae. Though he had got the muck off his body, there was some dirt clinging to his antennae that was blocking his sense of smell.

How similar we are to this bee! Each of us is this bee, with something within us that discolours everything we see. That dirt pervading our sense of smell is our bad attitude. The problem with this smell is that everyone except us knows it is the cause of our problems. Everyone else can clearly recognize the bad attitude that is affecting our lives, but we are so convinced that there is nothing wrong with our own perception, that we never try to rectify it.

We only need to pick up the mirror—remember the mirror? Only when we look hard at ourselves in the mirror do we recognize our bad attitude. A bad attitude is only one of the many faults that we need to work on. But it's the king of all faults. A lot of what we see in others exists in us. If we are worried about others judging us, it may be because we are judgemental. If we are worried about people gossiping about us, it may be because we gossip about others. Unless we understand our own realities, we will never understand other people's realities. The kind of person we are, strongly influences the way we look at others.

A survey in the journal *PLoS One** led to the surprising finding that only 53 per cent of our friendships are reciprocated! That is, more than half the time, your friendliness is not reciprocated. What this means is that while you may think that a particular person is your best friend, more than half the time, that person may not consider you a friend at all. This conclusion is not just from modern surveys, but is also validated by history. Let me tell you a story that provides an insight into how far back this theory goes. Just after the Kurukshetra war, Bhima was strolling around in the kingdom when he came across a peculiar problem. He found a villager crying, with five pots strewn around him. When asked why, the villager said that he was facing a big problem. He had filled a large pot with water and then emptied the contents of that pot into four smaller pots. But when he refilled the large pot with water from the four smaller pots, only half the big pot was filled. Where did the rest of the water go? Bhima was intrigued by this phenomenon. He took the matter to his wise brother Yudhishthira. Yudhishthira smiled and explained that this was a sure sign of Kaliyuga approaching. In this age, when you love someone with all your heart, you can only expect half the love in reciprocation. Only half of all friendships will be reciprocated in this age.

---

*   Cromm, Cari. 'Half of Your Friends Probably Don't Think of You as a Friend', *The Cut*, 6 May 2016, https://www.thecut.com/2016/05/half-of-your-friends-probably-dont-think-of-you-as-a-friend.html

Isn't that bang-on? Exactly what the modern survey concludes? Now the question is, why do people not reciprocate? It is easy to blame it on the age or on the growing selfishness in this world, on so many factors, but it is very difficult to accept that the reason why people don't reciprocate enough is possibly due to one's own bad attitude and shortcomings, which we are often unwilling to admit and rectify. It is possible that it is our own self which is the cause of this lack of reciprocity.

Here are some thoughts on why your friends may not be reciprocating your love and friendship. See where you stand on the qualities that make you a friend worth having:

- ✓ *Are you trustworthy?* To begin with, if a friend shares personal information with you, would you tell ten other friends because you can't resist gossiping? Well, that's not going to win you friends. So the question to ask yourself is—can you keep secrets? A good friend does not reveal secrets, come what may. Nor can you blackmail your friends by threatening to leak their secrets if they disagree with you at any point.
- ✓ *Are you constantly judging others?* Are you critical of your friend/s for their clothes, their choices, their decisions? No, good friends don't do that either. It is always best to avoid giving unsolicited opinions and judgements unless asked for. It makes your friends comfortable to know they have your support even if you do not totally agree with them.
- ✓ *Are you a good listener?* What really helps strengthen friendship is this very simple habit which, even though

it is simple, it is not practised often enough. Why so? Because we all have the urge to speak more than the urge to listen. Most of us like the sound of our own voices. But hey, everybody may not be interested in hearing repeatedly about your boss, your dog and your blood report. Give others a chance to speak, too. Remember what they say: we have one mouth but two ears.

✓ *Are you very possessive?* I know it is natural to be possessive of your friends, but monopolizing your friend's time or giving them no space to do anything without you is a recipe for disaster. I know of many friendships ruined between the best of friends because one friend becomes extremely possessive of the other, throwing a temper tantrum every time the other meets or spends time with their other friends or acquaintances.

✓ *Do you take time out to help your friends?* At the other end of the spectrum are those who fail to turn up for important life events like weddings. However busy you may be, making time for events that matter to your friends should be top priority.

✓ *Are you always distracted?* In the twenty-first century, we have one more rift-causing weapon that was not there earlier: the cell phone! How often do you check your phone for messages even when with your friends? Texting and tweeting when you are with your friends can be seen as offensive. You're sending a subtle message that you have more important things to do. Friends deserve to have your attention just as you deserve theirs. That's a no-brainer!

✓ *Are you competitive about everything?* Another modern bane of friendships is excessive competition. When we are in the race to win, there are no friends and no well-wishers, only competitors. Competing with friends takes the joy out of friendship. Friendship is all about cooperating and sharing, cheering for each other and celebrating each other's wins, not about wanting to win each and every time. If you are the competitive kind, watch out: it may get in the way of your friendships.

✓ *Do you distance yourself from your friends when you are in a relationship?* Many friendships go downhill when one friend gets romantically involved and their priorities change. It's natural to want to spend your time with your partner or date, but don't forget that it is your friends who pick you up when a romantic relationship falls apart. Snubbing your friends while you're dating will, sooner or later, leave you without friends.

✓ *Do you constantly expect your friends to foot the bill after drinks and food?* This is a no-brainer but is still important to state. No one will want to hang out with you if they find out you are a freeloader or you take advantage of their friendship. Friendship calls for generosity—of the heart and of the wallet, too. Keep your fist too tightly closed and you may find yourself sitting at the table alone.

✓ *Do you keep score?* In junior school, I kept track of how many times my best friend came to my home and how many times I had to go to his house. Believe me, that's not good for a healthy friendship. Fortunately, we devised a way to stop this habit of keeping score. What did we do? We took turns visiting each other! Today, it could be about keeping score of how many posts you liked on FB and how many smileys your friend responded with. It is actually irrelevant, immaterial, insignificant and superficial, especially once you realize that true friendship runs much deeper.

✓ *Do you dominate your friends too much?* Is it my way or the highway for you? This habit may snowball into something more frightening when you want your friend to do only what you want to do and offer them no other option. A stubborn, uncompromising attitude quashes emotions and bulldozes any remnants of genuine friendship. It's healthy to give in as often as not. The balance of the two is absolutely crucial.

Here's a story of two friends in the Mahabharata that shows how many of these factors ruin a perfectly good relationship. There were two girls who were the best of friends. They loved each other's company dearly. Though born and raised in totally different homes, they always found reasons and ways to meet daily. One was the daughter of the king of the land, whose name was Vrishaparva. The other was the daughter of the guru and spiritual advisor to the king, whose name was Sage Shukracharya. The king's daughter was called Sharmishtha and the daughter of the sage was named Devyani. One day, as usual, the girls had gone out to frolic with their maids in the beautiful groves of the forest on the outskirts of the kingdom. An exquisitely beautiful lake in the forest was their favourite hangout. After playing for hours in the bowers of flowering plants, the girls would bathe in the cool waters of the lake. That day, when they came back from their bath, Devyani was so busy chatting that by mistake, she wore Sharmishtha's clothes. Suddenly, she felt a hard tug from behind her. Sharmishtha was pulling forcefully at her clothes. Only then did Devyani realize that the clothes she was wearing weren't hers. She quickly removed them and handed them to the furious Sharmishtha.

Suddenly, the light-hearted mood of the party changed to an uncomfortably serious one. Sharmishtha was glaring at Devyani. She launched into an attack, demeaning Devyani's social position along with her irresponsible behaviour. 'I may be your friend, but that doesn't mean you can take liberties with me. I am the king's daughter, after all,' she ranted. 'How dare you wear my clothes? I am friends with you, but doesn't mean that you assume we are equal in status.'

This came as a shock to Devyani. She wasn't the type to stay quiet at being insulted. She spun around sharply and stepped threateningly towards Sharmishtha. Her eyes widened in fury and she spoke in a harsh tone, 'We are Brahmins; how dare you insult me? My father advises your father and in that way, our race is superior to yours!'

On hearing this, Sharmishtha gave Devyani a hard shove. Devyani toppled over the edge of the well that they were standing near and fell into the dry well. The maids were aghast. But having no choice but to follow their mistress, they left the poor girl to face her own destiny, lying helpless in the well. Hours passed as Devyani's screams echoed through the forest. No one seemed to hear her. Occasionally, a wild animal would peep over the edge of the well to locate the source of the screams but would go away once they realized that she was out of their reach. None of them wanted to risk getting stuck inside the dry well for the sake of one skinny meal. Finally, a handsome face appeared at the edge of the well. Soon, the strong arms of that handsome person pulled Devyani out of the well. Devyani immediately fell in love with her hero, who was none other than King Yayati of the neighbouring kingdom!

Meanwhile, Sage Shukracharya had learnt of his daughter's plight through the maids who had reached the kingdom. But by the time he went to his daughter's rescue, Yayati had already saved her. Devyani was hurt and naturally, vengeful. She wasn't ready to enter the kingdom again. Seeing his daughter's mood, Shukracharya also refused to return. When the king of the Asuras, Sharmishtha's father, learnt the reason for the absence of his guru, he rushed to Shukracharya and prostrated himself before the sage. He begged him to come back to the kingdom. Realizing the magnitude of his daughter's error and the dangerous consequences of the lack of Shukracharya's sage advice and mystical strengths, the king repeatedly begged for forgiveness for his daughter's folly, and even admitted to being lower than the sage in status. The king may be superior in the eyes of the world, but to the king, his guru is always superior. Devyani, however, refused to relent. She wanted her former friend, Sharmishtha, to come and declare her inferiority in front of all their friends. Having no other option and considering the greater welfare of the kingdom, Sharmishtha accepted the demand to declare to the world that she was inferior to Devyani. Further bowing to Devyani's desire, King Vrishaparva declared that his daughter would act as a maidservant to Devyani for the rest of her life.

At that, Devyani smiled and Sharmishtha cried.

Soon, Devyani married King Yayati with the blessings of Shukracharya. Sharmishtha, now her maid, also accompanied her to Yayati's kingdom. Shukracharya had ensured that his son-in-law took a vow to remain monogamous and not to fall for the charms of Sharmishtha. Yayati assured him of his commitment to the relationship. A few years passed and Yayati began to feel attracted to Sharmishtha, who was given accommodation a little distance away from the palace. Through Sharmishtha, Yayati begot three children, unbeknown his wife. Unfortunately for him, one day, Devyani discovered this secret love affair. Deeply disturbed and offended, she summoned her father. Sage Shukracharya once again came to the rescue of his daughter. He cursed Yayati—since he could not control his lust, he would lose his youth and become old and senile immediately.

This is a great example of a friendship that fell apart due to bad attitudes. Every bad attitude that could possibly break a friendship was present in these two friends. There was little possibility of this friendship lasting for very long.

They were both too judgemental. They couldn't control the urge to speak on impulse. They were so absorbed in themselves that they just couldn't spare a moment to see the other person's point of view. They were competing with one another to win. The competitive spirit simmered for years. They were expecting to receive from the other, but were not ready to give an inch. They always kept score. And of course, they had the dangerous mindset of 'my way or the highway'. What happened to Sharmishtha and Devyani could happen to any friendship. Of course, this might seem like a rather extreme example and you might wonder who could be so petty and dramatic in today's times. But just look around you—you will find several Sharmishthas and Devyanis. God forbid, but they could be inside you too!

Let me tell you some interesting facts about the animal kingdom that will help you understand relationships better. There are three types of relationships that animals have that are very similar to the three categories of friendships that human beings have with one another.

- The first type is a parasitic relationship. The nature of a parasitic relationship is selfish. In the animal kingdom, we find a flea having a parasitic relationship with a dog. A parasite latches on to the host and sustains itself on the flesh and blood of the host. In parasitic relationships among human beings, a friend latches on to another friend and feeds off the friend in several ways. It's all about taking from the other person selfishly. There is no gain, whatsoever, for the host; they only lose what they have. In many parasitic relationships, the host may not even be aware of the parasite sucking away the vitality from the relationship.
- The second type is a commensalist relationship. In this type of relationship, the host is not harmed but doesn't

gain either. In the animal kingdom, there is a particular type of fish known as the sucker fish that attaches itself to the underbelly of a shark. When the shark eats something, the sucker fish feeds on the remnants. The sucker fish gets food and protection from the shark but the shark gets nothing out of this relationship, except, perhaps, the satisfaction that it is providing for someone small. In commensalist friendships, since there is no harm done, the host usually doesn't mind it. It at least leaves you with the satisfaction of having done something for another, who may be weaker or less fortunate than yourself.

- The third type is a mutualistic or symbiotic relationship. As the name indicates, both the parties gain and neither is abused. In the animal kingdom, when a crocodile requires food particles stuck in its teeth to be extracted, it relies on the plover bird. It waits with its mouth agape for the plover bird to pick bits of food out of its teeth and help it maintain dental hygiene. In turn, the crocodile provides the bird with a good meal. Thus, both benefit each other. While gaining from each other, neither party thinks of harming the other. The crocodile doesn't close its mouth while the bird is inside. In case of human beings, such a relationship results in the development of trust and long-term mutual benefit between two friends.

While mutualistic relationships are clearly the best of these three, they should ideally not be developed with the intention of deriving gains from the other person, but should be born of compassion and empathy towards one another. Exploitation is probably the worst type of abuse in relationships. Parasitic relationships are abusive, often disguised as friendship. Hence, neither should you be a parasite for another friend, nor should you allow a parasite to exploit your kindness. As soon as the spirit of a Devyani or a Sharmishtha enters our hearts, we become incapable of friendship.

Summary:

- Prepare yourself for friendship before expecting it from others.
- Your attitude towards others determines their attitude towards you.
- It's easy to see fault in others, but is difficult to see fault in oneself.
- Before using a grimy window or a distorted lens, clouded by the Zeus fault, to look at others, you must spend some time gazing at yourself through the mirror of self-reflection and introspection. When you take a hard look at yourself in the mirror, you realize that there are many aspects of yourself you need to work on before being able to develop meaningful friendships and qualify as a good friend.
- Unless we work on our bad attitude and develop the right attitude and mindset, genuine friendship will always elude us.

Activity

Are you prepared for friendship? Let's find out.

Give yourself 5 points for every 'a', 3 points for every 'b' and 1 point for every 'c' option.

1. A good friend confides to you about something embarrassing that has happened.
   a. You keep the information secret and confidential because you don't want to break the trust
   b. Tell your best friend and ask them to keep it confidential because you share everything
   c. You can't resist announcing it on social media for all to see

2. You're ready to go for a Page-3 party where you have been asked to bring along a friend. When your friend comes to pick you, they are dressed shabbily.
   a. You ignore their appearance and introduce them to everyone in the party because they are great nevertheless
   b. You feel embarrassed to be seen with them and stand away from them in the party
   c. You feign a headache and cancel the plan to go to the party

3. A friend is in great distress about a problem she is facing. While they are telling you about it,
   a. You hear them patiently with full attention

    b. You keep interrupting them to give advice or find faults

    c. Check your phone constantly for messages

4. Your best friend is going for a holiday with a group of friends to a place you have recently visited

    a. You are excited for them and give them tips on what to do and where to go

    b. Tell them it's a lousy place to visit so that they cancel the holiday

    c. You throw a tantrum about them going out with other friends and not giving you enough time

5. A very dear friend is celebrating their promotion at work by throwing a small party with people close to them

    a. You cancel your prior engagements to celebrate their success

    b. You make an excuse about working late, apologize and send them a gift

    c. You don't think its important to even acknowledge such useless parties

6. When you're with friends for dinner

    a. You love to talk and gossip with them

    b. You share social media posts on your phone since there isn't that much to talk about

    c. You use that time to answer your messages and emails

7. Your friend breaks the news that they have got admission into the university that you were hoping to get into
    a. You feel elated and excited for your friend
    b. You surely feel happy but wonder why it wasn't you instead
    c. You are so upset you don't talk to them for days

8. You're in a dilemma because you had planned on catching a movie at the mall with a friend but your partner is suddenly available and wants to meet
    a. You tell partner you already have plans
    b. You tell your friend that something urgent came up and you reschedule the plan for the movie
    c. You cancel the movie plan abruptly and rush to see your partner

9. When at restaurants or the movies
    a. You always insist on sharing the bill
    b. You wait for someone else to pay and offer to pay for yourself later
    c. You allow others to pay for you

10. Your gang of friends is divided between a movie and going bowling
    a. You are happy to go with what the majority wants as long as everyone is are together
    b. You insist on your choice
    c. When it's not where you want to go, you throw a fit and refuse to go with them

Score

37–50: Congratulations! You are a champion in the world of friendship. You can retain a serious friendship. You definitely can be a great friend and have great friends.

26–36: You are good! With a little effort you can become the best friend anyone can ever have in the world. As you prepare yourself further, the quality of your friendships will enhance and the quality of friendship you offer others will also exponentially grow.

10–25: You are struggling with being a true friend to others. With a little sincere effort you can qualify to be a good friend. Remember that friendship is not a skill but an attitude. The more you work on your attitude and mindset the better equipped you become to offer meaningful friendship to others.

3

Friendship and Empathy

For us to have good friends, we need to eliminate the Narcissus in us. A narcissist is someone who focuses on themselves too much. Narcissus is not just a character in Greek and Roman mythology, but a dangerous mindset that lives within each one of us. Okay, before I go ahead, let me share with you the fascinating story of Narcissus that made him so famous—or infamous—that his name became the English word for excessive self-love.

According to Greek mythology, Narcissus was the son of the river god Cephissus and the nymph Liriope. When he was born, the prophet Tiresias told his parents that the greatest enemy of the boy was he himself. He warned them to keep the boy away from himself. The parents were, naturally, confused by this instruction. How could anyone be his own enemy? And how does one keep someone away from their own self?

The meaning of this statement became clear only when he grew up into a handsome young man. He was so good-looking that men and women alike would fall in love with him. He had an uncaring, arrogant attitude that led him to reject the advances of everyone. He cared for no one except himself. One fine day, after he had turned sixteen, he ventured out into the woods. An extremely beautiful nymph named Echo fell in love with him. Highly enamoured with his beauty, she began to follow him, keeping a safe distance. After some time, Narcissus realized that someone was following him. He called out, 'Who's there?'

Wanting to play games with him, Echo responded with the same words, 'Who's there?' Narcissus walked away silently, unable to locate the source of the voice. After some time, he felt it again—surely, there was someone following him. He turned around and again asked, with a little more irritation, 'Who's there?' Echo repeated his words in the same voice and tone. But he still couldn't find the source. When the same thing had been repeated several times, Narcissus grew unhappy. When Echo realized that her innocent game was putting off her beloved, she decided to make an appearance to make up for her mistake. Walking right up to him, Echo smiled enchantingly. Narcissus hardly noticed her beauty. She poured her heart out and told him that she had fallen in love with him the moment she had set her eyes on him and now, she couldn't imagine having anyone else as her husband. Echo then stepped towards Narcissus to take him into her loving embrace, but he harshly shoved her out of his way and walked away with nothing but contempt for her.

Echo couldn't handle the rejection. She spent the rest of her life in agony in the forest. Slowly, she started waning away until only her ability to echo all sounds remained. The story of Echo and the harshness of the proud Narcissus travelled far and wide till it reached the ears of Nemesis, the goddess of revenge. She decided to punish Narcissus for his heartless folly and pride. The goddess of revenge somehow inspired him to walk into the forest along the path that led him to a crystal-clear lake. When Narcissus walked towards the lake, he saw his own reflection in the waters and instantly fell in love with the image he saw on its surface. Mesmerized by his own beauty, he kept staring at his reflection, unable to take his eyes off himself. He longed to hold himself, but alas! He was unable to embrace his reflection. His self-obsessive madness reached the point of complete insanity. When he finally realized that he would never be able to get the one person he loved so much, he jumped into the lake and drowned.

You might be wondering what kind of stupidity that was. Who could love himself so much? But I assure you that Narcissus is not dead. A small part of Narcissus is present in each of us. It is this part of us that doesn't allow us to have satisfying relationships. It's a part of us that is so self-obsessed that it just doesn't allow us to focus on others. It's a part of us that is staring so intensely at our own needs, interests and concerns that it doesn't bother to even glance at the needs, interests and concerns of those who love us or those we associate with. Narcissism creates lonely people. The sad part is that when kids today have a narcissistic mindset, they are considered cute. Parents pamper them and sometimes even give them whatever they want. But when adults develop the same narcissistic mentality, instead of being considered cute, they become less likeable. People abandon them to their lonely, private worlds built around self-worship.

The mindset of fixation on oneself manifests itself most intensely today in the selfie culture. Oblivious to their surroundings or whom they are with, you find people so obsessed with themselves that they take selfies everywhere, which they then post on social media to show off their lives. Many of them are fascinated by themselves without even realizing it. They may have a lot, but they may be hated a lot too because of this self-obsession. You might wonder why I am being so harsh on those who have this mindset. Is self-love wrong?

To understand where I am coming from, I need you to reflect on this from a totally different perspective. I am going to take you on a roller-coaster ride. I am going to tell you two mind-blowing stories that will alter your perspective. The first is the true story of Jonathan Pedley. Till 2002, he was a multi-millionaire but also a thief, an adulterer and an alcoholic, by his own admission.* In 2010, he gave it all away to live with orphans in Uganda. What happened to him is a heart-warming tale that now makes for an interesting read.

---

* Davis, Barbara. 'This millionaire's been a thief, adulterer and alcoholic. Now he's giving his fortune away to help African orphans. So do we believe him?', *Daily Mail*, 15 March 2010, https://www.dailymail.co.uk/news/article-1257982/Jonathan-Bennion-Pedley-thief-adulterer-alcoholic.html

Right from his schooldays, Pedley lied, cheated, stole and did whatever was needed to get what he wanted. In his own words, he lived a life centred on himself. His parents were hard-working, and since he was the oldest of six children, they sent him to the most expensive of boarding schools, which they thought would help him make something of his life. But life seldom works out as per our plans. He constantly felt inferior to the other kids, who were always loaded with cash and frequently indulged in drugs. That triggered a personality change and by the age of thirteen, he was drinking, smoking and stealing, from his parents to begin with—he hated them as well as their conservative lifestyle. And when he was expelled from school, he cut off his parents as well. For him, money was the most important pursuit in life, above petty things such as family, relationships, honesty and contentment. None of those mattered.

From his first job, he figured out how he could make money illegally: scams. They were the perfect way to add to his income. As a store manager, he would make it look like there had been refunds when there were none. He amassed several thousand pounds in his two years there. By nineteen, his crimes had escalated and he was earning up to 20,000 extra pounds a year. It wasn't enough because the yuppies he associated with had a lot more. His devious mind devised another scam to avoid rent for housing, which involved using his charm to pay rent for only one month but staying on for six months and then suddenly disappearing from the scene. In those six months, he would even sell the furniture of the house, which was never his to begin with!

Thus, he began by stealing from his parents, went on to steal from his employers and did not stop even at stealing from his girlfriends. Feigning love, he would borrow money from girls and then abscond, and this was when he was only twenty-two. Next, he married an elderly woman, not for love but for the convenience. By thirty, he had the dream life: his own flourishing business and everything that money could buy, mansions, cars, exotic holidays, but no peace. Something was missing in his life. He tried alcohol; he tried adultery; he even had an affair with his wife's best friend and ended up marrying her.

While his personal life was in a shambles, his professional life flourished. That made him more arrogant. Then came the moment that turned his life around. One day, in 2002, he got into his car at 5 a.m. after a long business meeting. He was drunk. He had a nearly fatal car accident, ramming his car head-on into a speeding van. He remained in a coma for six weeks. When he came out of it, he could see with only one eye and had many fractures. But his bones were not the only thing he had broken— what also broke was his zeal for life, his confidence, his entire personality. He continued to drink heavily and grew abusive with his family.

This went on till the day he met an old friend in church. That day, he discovered two things: divinity, which helped him give up his drinking habit, and a purpose, which changed his conscience. He was very inspired by his friend's commitment to serve orphaned kids in Uganda. So inspired, in fact, that in 2010, he announced that he would sell off his luxurious mansion in the UK and set up a charity organization in Uganda. He would shift base and stay there in mud houses alongside them. The British media found it hard to believe. Imagine, a man with a tainted past, boasting of convictions, fraud, alcoholism, affairs and almost dying in a drunken car crash, suddenly claiming to have turned over a new leaf. Who would have believed him? But this time, he did what he promised to do. He transferred all his money to Uganda to a charitable entity and moved there to spend the rest of his life serving the underprivileged and living in a small mud hut.

Would you call this a miracle? Yes, and why not? Miracles do happen in real life. All it takes is a change of perspective to turn your life around; a shift in your vision. The shift could be minor, but its impact is anything but that. All it took for Jonathon to shift from self-centredness to other-centredness was a change of perspective that one tragedy gave him.

However, not everyone needs to go through a tragedy to change their perspective. Sometimes, life brings about a change in special ways—the way it happened in Soma's life. This rich, young, carefree dude had a change of perspective when he happened to go and live for a few days with his best friend Harsha. Soma came from a prosperous middle-class family where all his needs were met without question. Although there was discipline, there was also a lot of indulgence. But his friend was not rich. His parents had to think twice before spending on anything for Harsha. And although he had everything he needed, he never owned the high-end, branded goods that Soma did. However, Harsha never complained and because he never complained, Soma didn't know that Harsha was not as rich as him. They were simply happy in each other's company and at an age where status and money were not as important as fun and togetherness in friendship.

One day, Harsha invited Soma to stay with him for a few days and he readily accepted, thinking it would be nice to spend a few days together and have non-stop fun. The first thing that struck Soma was Harsha's house. It The house was much smaller than his and Harsha had a room that was barely big enough for the two of them. Yet, it didn't seem to matter to Harsha. He happily showed him around without any trace of embarrassment. Soma wondered what he would have done in the same situation. He would have been extremely embarrassed and never called a friend home. But because Harsha was so comfortable, Soma also immediately felt at ease. The next strange experience he had was at lunchtime. His mother served them lunch herself. There was no help. It was all home-cooked food and she conversed with them about many things while they were all eating. He recalled his lunch at home: his servants normally served him food in their empty dining room, his mother was usually at work so there was no question of eating with her. Suddenly, he was reminded of a sentence he had read in a book: 'Families that eat together, stay together.'

For a moment, he felt a stab of pain. He was not quite sure what caused the pain, so he ignored it. He focused on the love and warmth in the house and its residents. The next day, Harsha's mother went to take care of her married sister, who was sick, so Harsha and his father were doing the household chores. Soma asked Harsha, 'Don't you feel bad doing all this when you could be spending this time playing games, watching TV or just having fun?' He was surprised to hear Harsha's reply. He said, 'Soma, in a family, everyone has to contribute and do whatever they can, whenever they can. Even if I do very little, it makes my parents very, very happy. When my mother returns to see the house neat and tidy, and the dinner cooked, she will hug all of us. It makes me feel good to make her happy.'

Soma felt a glow of warmth in his heart. He had never thought of making his parents happy; it was always about his own happiness for him. It was about how *they* could make *him* happy, but now he saw how the reverse was also important. He started to think about how he could make his mother happy.

He was eager to go back home now. As he was packing his bag on his last day at their house, he overheard Harsha talking to his mother. Harsha was saying, 'Mother, can we go to Europe this summer for our vacation? Soma goes there every year.' There was a pause before his mother replied, 'It doesn't help to compare—Rumi, who stays in the building next to ours, does not go for any vacation at all. Instead, let's look at our options. We can either go to a hill station or a beach in India. Now, which would you prefer?' And Harsha happily chose the beach because he loved swimming and boating. Soma thought, *had it been me talking to my mother, I would have brought the house down if my demands were not met. But this is so much better, to adjust and go with the flow.* He returned home a new boy. He had learnt about love, about being happy with what you have and the benefits of cooperating and 'adjusting'.

But wait a minute! You may be wondering why I told you two stories about changing perspectives when it is friendship that we are talking about. The answer is simple. Friendship begins when we get rid of our self-centred mindset. As long as we remain at the centre of our lives, making good friends is out of the question. Friendship begins only when we start putting other people at the centre of our lives. As long as we are focused on serving our own needs, interests and concerns, there is no time or desire to focus on the needs, interests and concerns of another person. When we look at life from the perspective of others, it appears very different. When you look at life from only your own perspective, you tend to expect everyone to cater to your needs, interests and concerns. Anyone who does that diligently then becomes your friend and anyone who threatens the fulfilment of your desires even remotely becomes your enemy. Those who are too blinded by their own significance in the world become insignificant in the eyes of others. How significant you are to others depends on how much significance you give to others. The problem in wanting others to be interested in you is that you forget that others are also interested mostly in themselves. However, if you carefully study the most successful people in the world, invariably, they are those who are genuinely interested in others.

Here is a story of a person who is a household name in India: J.R.D. Tata. His is one of the first names that come to mind in the context of leaders who are interested in the well-being of others. There is an interesting anecdote about him. A young girl, fresh out of engineering college, spotted an ad for a job vacancy. She was left feeling aghast at one of the conditions for applying for that post, which stated that the opening was for males only. In a fit of anger at the rampant gender discrimination, she wrote a letter to the chairman of the company complaining about it. Not really expecting much to happen, she soon forgot about it. But she was pleasantly surprised when she got a call for interview. She not only went to give the interview but was selected for the job as well. All of this happened only because the chairman of that company, the Tata group, J.R.D. Tata, thought it was important to address the concerns of that young woman. Only when she went to the factory did she realize that the job that she was selected for was at a factory production line where only men worked across shifts. She was now the only woman in her shift. That's when she truly realized the thought that the company had put into mentioning that condition. But anyway, while she worked there, she realized that everything in the organization reflected the magnanimity and character of its leader. J.R.D. Tata was not just a chairman; he had a heart that always put the concerns of others first. In this way, he made a place for himself in many hearts, because people never forgot the warmth of his touch in their lives.

On another occasion, after the girl had joined the company, she was waiting on the steps, late in the evening, for her husband to pick her up. J.R.D. Tata happened to spot her and insisted on waiting with her till her husband came because it was not safe for her to wait alone after office hours. He, the chairman of one of the biggest corporate houses in India, did not mind waiting on the steps, simply out of concern for an employee! He even sent a message for her husband that he should not keep his wife waiting again. Such acts of unselfish concern for others always stand out, separating the wheat from the chaff. There are thousands of people who find success, but there are only a few who are successful and yet unselfish. Interested not just in their own success but in others' success too, they make a difference to everyone they come across. Such other-centric people remain forever etched in the minds of those whose lives they touch.

You don't really need to impress anyone, you just need to let people know that you care. I am sure you've heard of the famous saying by former American president Theodore Roosevelt, 'People don't care how much you know until they know how much you care.' If you focus only on yourself, you can never build good friendships. Even animals in the jungle know that principle. Do you want to know how? Here is an amazing fable about how some animals may have discovered that.

An old crow was lonely. His family was no more and he had no friends. He would spend his days alone in his nest and leave only for a short duration in search of food. Though he was old, he was alert. One day, from inside his nest, he happened to see a man doing something suspicious under a tree nearby. A look at the man's expressions convinced the crow that he had a sinister motive. He had a huge net in his hand that he threw expertly, spreading it on the ground and covering a large area. The crow knew that he was definitely up to some mischief. He crouched in his nest, trying to avoid the gaze of this mischief-monger, and saw that the man was sprinkling grains inside the net. Having finished his job, he went and hid behind a tree. The crow panicked when he understood his evil intent.

Within a few minutes of laying the snare, a king pigeon flew past with his flock. The grains gleamed from below and were inviting them to a juicy treat. The king pigeon swooped down, focusing his entire attention on the strewn grains. His flock followed their leader. None of them could even see the net on which they were standing, pecking at the grains. Only when one of them tried to fly away did they all realize that their feet were entangled in the mesh of the net. They all panicked as soon as they understood what this meant. Great joy lit up the hunter's face at the sight of what he had gained—an entire flock! The crow, meanwhile, looked on helplessly.

As the hunter ran towards them, happy at the many meal portions that he had trapped in one go, the net began to rise skywards. What was going on? The hunter began to scream helplessly at the net, which moved higher and higher into the sky until it was completely out of his reach. The crow was impressed with the king pigeon's quick wit. The intelligent bird had instructed his flock to pick up the net in their beaks and fly upwards together. With their collective strength, they were able to carry the heavy net away. After flying a short distance, the pigeons began to tire out. Unused to carrying such weight, they had to catch their breath. Though the immediate danger was taken care of, they were still far from being free.

Their feet were still trapped in the net. An idea struck the king pigeon, who instructed his flock to fly to a nearby tree. The crow was surprised to see the pigeons return to the same area where the net was originally laid. But he decided to observe carefully before passing judgement on their intelligence.

As soon as the trapped pigeons landed, they began to call out in unison, 'Hiranya! Hiranya!' Out came a tiny mouse from a rathole somewhere in the roots of a gigantic tree. Even before the king pigeon had said anything, Hiranya the mouse began to cut through the net with his teeth. One by one, the pigeons were set free to soar the clear skies, breathing in their freedom.

The crow was amazed by the friendship between the pigeon and the resourceful mouse. Suddenly, he realized that he really missed having company—all he needed was a good friend. And who could be a better friend than the mouse he had just seen in action? He was so excited to befriend the mouse that he swooped down from his nest on the tree straightaway to introduce himself to the kind mouse. Seeing a natural enemy swoop down towards him in that way, the mouse scrambled back to the safety of his hole. When he noticed the mouse was missing, the crow began to call out his name in a gentle voice. 'My dear Hiranya, I am Laghupati, the friendly crow. I am looking for a good friend. Seeing you help the pigeons, I have concluded that you will make a great friend. I promise you that I will do my best to make this friendship invaluable for you too. I am old and have now turned vegetarian, so you have nothing to fear.'

The mouse reluctantly agreed to meet the crow once to see if he wanted to befriend him. They agreed to meet over dinner. The mouse didn't want to meet either at the crow's nest or at his own house, but chose a third venue. They agreed upon the place where the hunter had thrown lots of rice. That would make for a great dinner and also a safe zone for the mouse to escape if he felt threatened by the crow. Hiranya and Laghupati hit it off right from the beginning. They became so comfortable with each other that they soon became the best of friends and were with each other all the time. One day, the crow suggested that they go for an outing. He was tired of living in the same place and needed a break. The mouse agreed, but also told him about his inability to travel long distances. The crow suggested that they visit his old friend Mandharka, the tortoise. Though he was slow in his movements, he had lived a very long time and so would have a great many stories to entertain and educate them with. Laghupati even offered to carry the little Hiranya in his beak to the distant land.

Off went the two friends on the long journey that took them a few days, and finally, they were in the company of the wise old tortoise. The three grew to love each other's company. The stories the tortoise shared with them were entertaining, but his shortcoming was that he spoke very slowly. They discussed their strengths and weaknesses. The tortoise showed them the power of his hard, thick shell. They were amazed. The mouse displayed the advantages of being so small. The crow showed them the advantage of being able to see things from a different perspective and soon, the three of them became inseparable.

One day, they had an unexpected guest. Running at a great pace, a beautiful deer sprinted towards them and stopped right in their midst. He was in great fear. Sweating and trembling, he kept throwing startled glances behind him. Someone was following him. The only word that could escape from the deer's mouth was 'hunters'.

That was enough to alert the three friends about the approaching danger. Immediately, the crow flew high up to a perch on a tall tree to survey the area. When he saw that the hunters chasing the deer had gone far away in another direction, he came back and reported the good news to his friends. The deer thanked the three friends for supporting him. They welcomed him and shared their meal with him. They offered him their company and shelter till he recovered from his wounds and exhaustion. The crow kept a vigilant watch on their enemies. The tortoise entertained them with his wisdom and the mouse offered words of solace. The deer was touched by their kindness and generosity; he decided to start living with them. The four friends gave each other privacy and space all day. But every evening, they got together to share their learnings and have a wonderful time.

One evening, the deer didn't turn up. Since it was a moonlit night, visibility was not bad. The crow flew up to the top branch of the tallest tree and scanned the area. After looking in all directions, Laghupati saw a dark mass by the riverside. He realized that it was at the exact spot where his deer friend would go to drink water. Alerting his friends, the crow flew to that spot, only to find the deer struggling in a huge net. The more he struggled, the tighter the net got. The crow once again found himself helpless. He had always had a fear of nets and after seeing the pigeons struggling, he had decided to stay far away from them. But that reminded him of his friend, Hiranya, the mouse, who he knew had the solution to this problem. Off he flew and returned in a jiffy with the saviour on his back. The very next moment, the mouse began his nibbling and the net began to loosen up. Soon, the deer was standing, freed from the dangerous snare.

Meanwhile, the slow tortoise caught up with them. He had been too worried about his friend to stay in the safety of his home. Though it took him longer to reach the spot, and his friend had been freed by that time, he still felt it was worth coming here rather than sitting and worrying there. The four friends were happily reunited again now. Embracing one another and appreciating the hero of the day, the capable mouse, they laughed in joy. Suddenly, they realized that they were right in the middle of danger zone. The hunter could be coming anytime. They rushed away from the scene. In a matter of minutes, the crow, the mouse and the deer were back in their abodes. But the tortoise would take his own sweet time to return. An hour passed and yet, the tortoise hadn't returned. Even if he walked slower than he did, it shouldn't take him that long to return. Sensing that some danger had befallen him, the three friends left their homes and ventured out into the forest again, looking for their thick-shelled friend. They got the scare of their lives when they saw the evil hunter carrying the tortoise in his net slung on his back. The helpless look in the eyes of their friend brought tears to their eyes. Right then, the mouse had a brilliant idea. He told the deer to go a little farther ahead and play dead. The crow should sit on the dead deer's face and act as if it were pecking at the eyes. The deer was not at all happy to be lying in the path of the hunter from whose snare he had just escaped. But wanting to save his trapped friend, he restrained his panic and cooperated. Though the deer and the crow had no idea what the mouse meant to do, they followed his instructions.

Seeing a dead deer on the pathway, the hunter dropped the tortoise with a thud. The protective shell of the tortoise cushioned his fall. As soon as the deer saw the hunter approach, he got up and ran for his life. The hunter chased him frantically. In the meantime, the mouse rushed towards the trapped tortoise, cut through the net and released him. The deer took the hunter on a good, long chase. That gave the slow tortoise enough time to make his escape. Finally, the deer managed to trick the hunter and disappear from his sight. Having lost the deer, the hunter came back for the tortoise but found it missing. He was totally confused. He felt that there was some magic at work in this forest that thwarted all his endeavours.

Finally, the four friends were back together and celebrating the spirit of friendship that had saved their lives. The deer and the tortoise praised and thanked the mouse again and again for his heroic efforts and keen intelligence, which saved them. The crow, feeling left out, chipped in that if it wasn't for his observation, the mouse wouldn't have been able to help them at all. All of them laughed loudly and acknowledged the crow's contribution. The four friends decided that no matter what, they would never break the friendship up and would always remain together. They realized that their friendship grew because it had developed to focus not on their selfish needs, but on the needs of the others. A friend who helps in need is a friend indeed.

A self-centred person remains hungry for love, restless for attention and lonely without company. Like a small child, they are at peace only when people give them attention. If only they could understand that the more attention they demand, the less people feel inclined to give it. What one needs to realize is we are not hungry for attention, but for love. Without loving friends, we feel lonely and depressed. As American Baptist minister Joseph F. Newton put it, 'People are lonely because they build walls instead of bridges.' Friendship is all about surrendering your ego to focus on the relationship. In fact, the ego is often the greatest obstacle to friendship. Egoistic people put themselves first. This unhealthily singular focus on oneself comes at the cost of others. They use everyone else to accomplish their goals. Everyone they befriend is simply a puppet that dances to their tunes and is used to execute the master plan of their life. An egoist thinks so little of others that he doesn't even acknowledge their views. In their mind, when you don't even exist except as a tool for them to use to meet their own ends, how can your views matter to them?

Life begins only when we acknowledge that the world doesn't revolve around us. The sooner we get over ourselves, the more friends we can make. Only when we begin to value other people do we truly understand that everyone can teach us something and everyone has something valuable to share.

Another important point to remember is that emotionally weak people love themselves. While your Intelligence Quotient determines how much you know, your Emotional Quotient determines how well you connect. High EQ does not necessarily accompany high IQ. In fact, in many cases, your IQ eats up your EQ. Many highly intelligent people end up being lonesome. This is simply because they have invested all their energies in developing their IQ, often at the risk of neglecting the development of their EQ. EQ is crucial to managing your own emotions as well as those of others. For success in any relationship, one has to have a healthy EQ. Your EQ allows you the flexibility to think beyond yourself. It allows you to adapt to new forms of thinking and to see the world from others' perspectives. It allows you to accept and value others' opinions. It allows you to think beyond yourself. It allows you to become a balanced human being who knows how to balance your own needs with the needs of the people important to you. A highly developed EQ allows you to have a healthy reserve of psychological energy that brings you peace of mind.

The best way to focus on others is to get out of your own world and step into another's. When you remain in your own small world, all you see is your own self and your own problems. Everyone simply becomes a visitor or helper, who you presume is there to help you deal with your problems. When you get out of your own world, you can finally change your focus. When you return to your own world with this altered perspective, it begins to look very different. I am going to share a story of two friends who spent time with one another, leaving behind their own worlds and stepping into the other's world. By doing that, they could both see each other from a changed perspective. Their friendship lasted a lifetime and has gone on to become an example for the world to emulate.

This is a story from the Bhagavat Purana. It's the story of the extraordinary friendship between Krishna and Sudama. Often quoted as one of the most significant stories about true friendship in the Indian epics, it teaches us invaluable lessons. There are two parts to this story. The first part is about the initial phase of their friendship, in their childhood. This is the part where Krishna leaves his world and enters Sudama's. The second part describes the mature phase of their friendship, in their adulthood, the part in which Sudama leaves his world and enters Krishna's. But there is a common thread that links both parts and which forms the crux of their beautiful friendship. You need to first hear both stories to appreciate that essence.

Krishna and Sudama first met in the gurukul run by their teacher, Sandipani Muni. As was the custom, they stayed at the gurukul for the entire duration of their education. Though raised in totally different situations, this helped them bond very closely and become the best of friends. They lived in their guru's simple, pristine ashram and participated in all the activities enthusiastically. Along with their knowledge of the different subjects being taught there, the love they had for each other also grew. Soon, they were inseparable.

One day, Sandipani Muni sent the two boys to the forest to fetch firewood. Krishna and Sudama happily went and began collecting firewood diligently. Once they had gathered enough wood, they set off for the gurukul. They wanted to cover the forest path before sunset, or else they would be lost in the utter darkness of the forest. As they were making their way back with the bundles of firewood, a storm broke. All of a sudden, the forest grew utterly dark. It began to pour so heavily that it was impossible to see anything. The two friends took shelter under a huge tree in the forest. Though extremely hungry and tired, they knew there was no way out of the forest till the storm subsided.

When their teacher came looking for the missing boys the next morning, the scene before him brought a smile to his face. He saw the two boys seated on a thick branch of a tall tree, holding each other's hands tightly. Under their other arms were bundles of wood they had collected to bring back to their teacher. They had neither deserted each other, nor neglected their duties towards their teacher. They had stood for each other during trying times.

Childhood friendships may make for very sweet memories but they are often forgotten over the passage of time. However, the friendship between this duo remained exactly the same even with the passing years. Though they didn't meet at all for decades, the day they did, it felt like they had never been apart. Their affection for each other had remained unaltered. Sudama grew up to be a pious brahman, who lived a simple life in poverty but in satisfaction. He had a beautiful, devoted wife and several children. Krishna, on the other hand, grew up to have a great many adventures and, eventually, went on to become the king of the exquisitely beautiful island of Dwarka. He was married to the most beautiful princesses from around the world and his principal wife, Rukmini, was one of the most celebrated beauties in all the land.

It so happened that once, Sudama's wife, in a state of helplessness, urged her husband to meet his friend Krishna. She thought Krishna would surely understand the poverty-stricken plight of his friend and lend a helping hand in some way to help make their lives easier. Sudama was excited at this proposal, not so much because of the possibility that his poverty might end but at the possibility of spending time with his most beloved childhood friend. The first thing Sudama told his wife was that if he was to meet Krishna, he wished to carry a gift for him. His wife was surprised. Here she was, urging him to go and ask for help, but her husband was thinking about giving instead of receiving!

Somehow, he managed to make the arduous journey from his small village to Krishna's opulent island-city. He didn't even expect to be remembered. *Who remembers a poor school friend?* he thought. But to his pleasant surprise, not only did Krishna remember him, he took special care of Sudama. Krishna even washed his poor friend's weathered feet with his own hands. He put aside all his kingly duties for the few days that Sudama stayed with him in Dwarka and totally focused on providing the best hospitality and care to his friend. In fact, Krishna got his entire family involved in providing the most luxurious, comfortable and loving stay to his best friend. They spent time together, having soul-searching conversations and revisiting the memories of their sweet childhood days.

After spending some time together happily, Krishna asked Sudama if he had brought any gift for him. Surely, he would have got something. Though Sudama had brought a gift, he was hesitant to offer it to Krishna. Surrounded by the opulence of Krishna's kingdom, he felt that the packet of puffed rice in his possession was too inadequate a gift. Not even the lowest of maids or sentries in such a palace would so much as look in the direction of that rice. Sudama tried his best to hide the packet from Krsihna. Becoming aware of his friend's predicament, Krishna ran towards him and forcibly snatched his gift. Then, like an excited child who receives his birthday present, Krishna immediately dug his hand into it, picking up a handful of the flat rice. When he took the first bite of that coarse rice, Krishna had to close his eyes to savour the unbelievable flavour of that simple food. He realized soon enough that he had simply tasted Sudama's love for him. He had to admit that this was much more than the love that he had experienced from many of his closest family members. He felt ashamed that compared to the love that Sudama had offered him, there was hardly anything he could give him in return. The only thing he felt he could offer his friend was gratitude, and so, Krishna shed tears of gratitude and love.

Sudama decided against asking Krishna for any favours when he realized how deep their friendship ran. They were both so satisfied with their loving exchanges that as Sudama walked back home with special memories, even if still with an empty pocket, he felt grateful to Krishna for not allowing wealth to take precedence over their friendship. Sudama had decided to focus on Krishna and Krishna had decided to focus on him in return. They put aside any other considerations and factors that could create a rift between them.

Be it cultural differences, socio-economic differences, status or anything else tangible, they chose to remain focused on the one fact that they needed each other and were interested in each other's well-being. Sudama returned a happier man, having understood what true friendship meant; though Krishna had not given him any wealth in person, he found that he had had a huge sum sent to his house directly. Sudama was overwhelmed at the amount of wealth Krishna had showered on his family. But he decided to value and cherish only the wealth of their love and friendship.

Friendship, therefore, is a responsibility that necessitates that you put the other before yourself. By getting out of their own worlds, Krishna and Sudama were able to see life from each other's perspectives. They could empathize with each other better when they took the time to understand the other's situation. They worked on making the other person feel important. It wasn't a grand display but a small act of kindness, performed sincerely and with great feeling. When positive experiences are created for another person simply out of a feeling of charity, rather than sincerity, those experiences simply touch the other person's mind. They don't even come close to touching their heart. But when every endeavour to please the friend you love so dearly is undertaken with honesty and selflessness, the experience remains etched in the walls of your friend's heart forever.

So now you might wonder, who is a true friend? This is eloquently answered in the following Sanskrit verse:

Papaan nivarayati yojyate hitaaya
guhyani guhati gunaan prakatikaroti
aapdantam cha na jahaati dadaati kale
sanmitralakshanamidam pravadanti santah

(A good friend is one who removes your defects, offers good advice, directs you to the righteous path, praises your good qualities, never abandons you in times of need and supports you in every way possible. This is the conclusion of learned men)

Only when you believe in the best in people, will you see the best in people; when you take an interest in people, people will take an interest in you; when you prioritize other people over yourself, people will prioritize you over themselves; when you make sacrifices, people will make sacrifices for you; when you encourage people to talk about themselves, people will encourage you to talk about yourself.

Well, that's a tall order. But we can begin by taking small steps. Next time you meet someone with whom you don't really like to interact, try this. Ask him about himself, his difficulties and encourage him to talk. Take an interest in hearing him. Ask him if he needs your help. Be genuine in your interaction. You will observe that all the reasons you had to avoid this person will melt away and he will also warm up towards you. When you radiate positive vibes, you impel others to react positively too.

Friendship is not a one-way street on which you can ride alone like a king. Friendship is a two-way highway where, on both sides, love and communication must flow unhindered.

Summary:

- Understand the value of empathy, to put yourself in the other's shoes.
- Learn to put your friends' needs before your own when they need your support.
- Value friendship above all.

Activity

Match the names from the stories in Chapter 2 (Column A) to what each one represents (Column B).

Column A	Column B
1. Narcissus	Had nothing but gratitude to offer a friend
2. Jon Pedley	Small but always useful to friends
3. Crow	Changed perspectives by observing
4. Mouse	Learnt to be satisfied with what one has rather than what one doesn't
5. Tortoise	Ready to take risks for friends
6. Dear	Insensitive to others
7. Krishna	Lonely and looking for a friend
8. Sudama	Slow but a wise friend
9. J.R.D.Tata	From selfishness to selflessness
10. Soma	Feels friendship is more valuable than all the wealth in the world
11. Harsha	Concerned about others, whoever they may be

Check your answers:

Column A	Column B
1. Narcissus	Insensitive to others
2. Jon Pedley	From selfishness to selflessness
3. Crow	Lonely and looking for a friend
4. Mouse	Small but always useful to friends
5. Tortoise	Slow but a wise friend
6. Dear	Ready to take risks for friends
7. Krishna	Feels friendship is more valuable than all the wealth in the world
8. Sudama	Had nothing but gratitude to offer a friend
9. J.R.D. Tata	Concerned about others, whoever they may be
10. Soma	Changed perspectives by observing
11. Harsha	Learnt to be satisfied with what one has rather than what one doesn't

4

Friendship Is a Responsibility, Not a Competition

Two good friends were walking through a jungle. It was extremely quiet. Even the smallest sounds of their footsteps were amplified manifold. Suddenly, they heard a heavy rustling somewhere behind them. When they turned around, trembling, they got the shock of their lives! They were horrified to see a grizzly bear running towards them. The friends broke into a run, and a chase ensued between man and beast. In the middle of this intense chase, one of the friends stopped suddenly, took off his backpack and removed a pair of running shoes from it. Since he was taking his time putting them on, the second friend asked if he was out of his mind, stopping to wear shoes when the bear was just around the corner. 'No matter what you do, you can't outrun a bear,' he said. With a smile, the boy putting on the shoes answered that he knew very well that he couldn't outrun the bear—all he had to do was outrun his friend!

Such is the mindset of competition: save yourself first and at any cost. Such competition stifles friendship and promotes animosity. Sadly, we live in a highly competitive world where only the fittest survive. In this fight for survival against so many people and so many odds, shouldn't there be some people in our lives whom we don't have to and don't want to compete against? People who can be our refuge from the exhausting competitive spirit we exhibit against the rest of the world? If we begin to compete with the very people who are supposed to be our refuge, we will become drained, lonely and miserable. Only friendship can be a safe haven where exhausting competition does not exist. What exists instead is kindness, sharing and love.

Unfortunately, the spirit of competition is so deeply ingrained in us that we do not even understand what sharing means. Sharing begins with caring. Caring begins with listening. And listening is anything but easy. Listening is not just about hearing spoken words but also understanding the other person's unspoken feelings. Most people hear with uncaring ears; to listen, you need not just open ears but also a caring heart. Those who are full of themselves seldom have any space to accommodate others' feelings. Only when sharing becomes the basis of friendship can a spirit of competition be replaced with that of love.

Let me tell you another story to illustrate my point. During the French revolution, there was an acute shortage of food. The queen of France was informed that people did not have bread to eat and were starving. But she lived such a luxurious life herself that she was totally disconnected from the struggles of the common man. She heard the words but couldn't listen to their import. She was hearing, not listening, and this is why she replied that if they didn't have bread to eat, 'let them eat cake'. When you are so full of yourself, you have no space for anyone else. When you don't care for the other person, how are you going to listen to them and if you don't listen, how are you going to share their joys and sorrows?

Most people are highly self-absorbed and place their agenda ahead of others'. No matter the consequence, their personal agenda is foremost in their minds. With such a mindset, listening to another's viewpoint becomes very difficult. Something similar happened with two friends, Amit and Sid. Amit asked Sid to meet him for coffee a couple of times and Sid refused. Amit thought Sid did not want to meet him anymore. But actually, Sid was suffering from depression because he was about to lose his job and did not want to meet anyone in that state. But Amit was so focused on himself and his own ego that he failed to focus on Sid's non-verbal feelings. As long as it's about going out for coffee, it's fine, but not being able to listen to another's feelings can sometimes become a question of life and death. How? Here's another story that will explain.

Malati was very harsh in her tone and in her dealings. Her husband, Rajaram, had to tolerate a lot of it. Being soft-spoken and gentle, he felt that while his wife may be insensitive, she was not a bad person. He was a very successful businessman and decided to focus on expanding his business rather than trying to rectify his wife's bad attitude. He simply complied with Malati's every desire so that there would be peace at home. One day, the couple was sitting together and dining. Rajaram noticed two ants next to his plate. He overheard their conversation. If you are wondering how a human could overhear the conversation of ants, let me tell you that Rajaram had a special boon bestowed on him by a powerful sage that enabled him to understand the language of any living being. In the conversation he heard, one ant was telling the other ant that the plate belonged to him and that anything that fell from that plate also belonged to him. Rajaram couldn't contain his laughter at the cute bullying that was going on even in the ant kingdom. There were bullies everywhere. It was very funny to Rajaram.

However, his wife had other thoughts. She wasn't happy to see him laughing privately about something that she wasn't a part of. She asked him to tell her the reason for his laughter. That's when he realized the folly of having laughed in her presence. He could not, of course, tell her that he had heard the ants speak. The sage who had blessed him had also warned him that if he ever spoke about these animal conversations with anyone, he would die immediately. Wanting, naturally, to live, Rajaram kept his mouth sealed. His silence had an adverse effect on Malati's behaviour. She began to doubt Rajaram's loyalty towards her. She felt that maybe he had another woman on the side whose loving words he remembered and laughed. She kept pestering him to tell her and he kept refusing to speak. Soon, she began to yell and scream so loudly that her shrill voice reverberated all over the house. Rajaram fell at her feet and told her that if he revealed the reason behind his laughter, he would die instantly.

She said never mind if he died, she had to know why he laughed. Rajaram was shocked and a great realization dawned on him: were her feelings more important than his *life*? What was the point in living with someone who only cared for her own feelings?

What Rajaram experienced is something many of us do in our lives too: insensitivity, a lack of empathy. Self-absorption makes people insensitive to the impact of their words on another's heart. Unmindful of consequences, the ego becomes a wall that prevents you from understanding another person's feelings. Even if you put your ego aside and begin taking baby steps in trying to listen to the other person's feelings, there are other problems that come in the way. The first is distraction. There's plenty of that around us, beginning from our very dear mobile phones! As we try to listen attentively to what the other person is trying to convey, the cell phone keeps beeping and buzzing, demanding our attention. Somehow, when you finally drag your attention away from the cell phone screen, there are other screens trying to catch your eye.

If you do manage to overcome all these distractions, a closed mind poses the next obstacle in listening. What is a closed mind? It is a mind that believes it knows everything and therefore, does not need to waste time hearing what the other person has to say. Even before it is said, the closed mind knows it. A closed mind leads to closed ears. And God forbid, if any words of criticism fall on our eardrums, we switch off our hearing and switch on the defensive mode.

Once the self-defence mode is on, it's a one-way street. We cannot hear anything at all except our own voice struggling to justify our actions. We don't think twice before savagely dismissing the other person's feelings in trying to protect our own prestige. If we bypass the self-defence mode, we take the route of assumptions. And false assumptions lead to false conclusions.

With so many genuine obstacles to listening, how can two souls have a deep, meaningful dialogue and not self-focused mental monologues?

Here's a key prescription to salvage your friendships: convert your enthusiasm to speak into an enthusiasm to listen. We should be just as eager to understand what the other person is trying to say as to make a witty reply. When you listen with an open heart, people are willing to open their hearts to you too. And when they open their hearts to you, your heart glows with warmth. During painful periods, when emotions are chaotic, people are most in need of an audience, a good friend who has the patience to listen. Such emotionally significant events should be viewed as gardens in which the flowers of friendship can blossom, be it joy or sorrow, success or failure, victory or defeat, gain or loss. At such times, someone who is available to listen sincerely and empathetically will gain a lifetime friend. I suggest trying to listen like this the next time a friend needs your ear. You will be surprised by their genuine gratitude towards you!

As Kahlil Gibran said, 'Friendship is a sweet responsibility, never an opportunity.' If you are a true friend, you should not expect anything in return when you choose to provide support; it is not an opportunity to gain something in the future by investing something in the present. The key to a lasting friendship is in having deep feelings and empathy towards your friend. Friends who support us are those who are present not only through our ups and downs but also through our 'normal' periods. They remind us that life is not to be lived for oneself. They push us to go beyond our own needs, interests and concerns.

Do you feel your support is misconstrued and you get dominated? Many people prefer not to help others because of a fear of being taken for granted or taken advantage of. Supporting others does not mean jeopardizing your interests, but being there for your friend when they need you.

A marriage proposal from USA had turned Simran's life upside down. Although it was an exciting prospect, she was apprehensive about leaving her elderly parents behind. *Everything will be alright*, people told her. She had relatives who lived around her parent's place so that was one safety net. And she could fly down to India once a year. She had mixed feelings about the marriage proposal—she was happy to begin a new life in a country people dream of going to, but was sad at having to leave her parents behind.

She went ahead with the match anyway. Life was good for a few years . . . till her parents' health took a turn for the worse. Age caught up with them. While one had been suffering from Parkinson's, the other had developed dementia and other age-related issues. They could not remember if they'd taken their medicines; they needed help walking from one room to another; the relatives who had promised their support had more pressing problems to handle. Simran had employed a full-time assistant to help them with their daily activities, but he could not be relied on for everything. She travelled to India whenever necessary, but the weather and food there did not suit her after a few years away, so she was able to visit only infrequently. But her parents were alone and helpless and she needed someone trustworthy to keep an eye on them. With no hope left, all she could do was pray.

One day, she heard from her best friend, Alisha, who had returned to India after living in Australia for a few years. She and Simran had been the best of friends since childhood. Speaking to her was like a rejuvenating, fresh breeze, erasing all exhaustion. They discussed their lives and everything else under the sun. Simran revealed to Alisha her anxieties about her parents. Alisha felt bad because she had spent many a happy day in Simran's house, enjoying the food that Simran's mother cooked. Her mother had been as loving towards Alisha as her own. Learning of their troubles made her feel very sad. She wanted to help her friend in some way. She quickly volunteered to go and meet her parents and see if they were well. Simran heaved a sigh of relief. She did not want to impose on her friend, but because it was Alisha who had suggested it, she immediately welcomed her support.

Alisha went over the same afternoon. She saw the assistant was not very particular about giving the couple their medicines on time. Explaining to him gently why he should be more careful, she herself organized the medicines in a dispensing box to make it easier for Simran's parents. She instructed other domestic aides to report to her in case of any problems. She kept Simran informed about what was going on and how she had instructed the staff to report to her to prevent them taking advantage of the senior citizens, who were incapable of protecting themselves. She would also drop in to check on them once a week. Simran was extremely grateful to Alisha. A friend in need was a friend indeed. Alisha had done for her what no one else was willing to do. In fact, she reflected, no one volunteered to help anyone anymore. Everyone was too busy to care about others. But thank God for a friend like Alisha, who made the effort to find time for friends when they needed her support the most. Simran had not asked Alisha for help, but Alisha had instinctively known that she needed it, and she was there for her. Simran would never forget that as long as she lived.

Friends like Alisha make us believe that selfless friendships do exist. In the words of British author Dorothy L. Sayers, 'Trouble shared is trouble halved.' Alisha may not have been able to solve Simran's problem, but she could share it. The Alishas of this world serve as reminders that each of us can be a gift to mankind if we wish to. We may not be able to transform the whole world at once, but we can certainly transform the world of one friend. And that is a significant accomplishment.

One of my favourite sayings is by Ruskin Bond, 'No words heal better than the silent company of a friend.' How true that is! Who would want to go through the roller-coaster of life alone? Even in the roller-coasters in theme parks, there are always two seats next to each other to allow people to experience the thrill of life completely, together, in company. On the roller-coaster of life, good friends support you not only during bad times but are also present in the good times. The one constant in the changing variables of life is a friend. Of course, we cannot promise our friend that we will remove their pain, but we can certainly relieve it by the power of our presence. Presence! A very strong word, indeed. Presence conveys the message, 'Don't give up, I am here with you.' That's all a friend sometimes needs. Can you think of a time you were present for a friend? Did it not change the dynamics of your friendship?

One such friendship is celebrated in the Mahabharata. Krishna called Draupadi his *sakhi* and Draupadi called him her *sakha*. This was the third level of friendship: they were priya sakhas. Krishna was always present in her life. Their friendship and commitment to each other were exemplary. At every instance in her life when she needed support, Krishna was there. Just like her husband Arjuna had a deep bond with Krishna, Draupadi too connected with Krishna deeply. Once, Krishna was flying kites on the terrace of their palace. Due to a sudden jerk, the kite string cut into Krishna's hand and it began to bleed profusely. While everyone else rushed to get medical help, Draupadi spontaneously tore off a corner of her sari and tied it to Krishna's hand to stop the bleeding. That spontaneous loving gesture moved Krishna and he promised to stand by her no matter what. And that he did diligently.

When Draupadi was being disrobed in the *asat sabha* or the nasty assembly hall, none of her husbands were able to help her. The elders in the family weren't able to help her either, nor were the thousands of citizens and onlookers. When she realized that it was vain to depend on any of these people, she turned her attention inwards and in the core of her heart, she found an answer. Intuitively, in every trying circumstance, she would turn to Krishna for support. He never let her down, and he came to her rescue in this one as well.

Once, when Draupadi was in the forest with her husbands, a great calamity befell them. It came in the form of Durvasa. Durvasa was an angry sage. He had made his appearance unannounced. If he had come alone, it wouldn't have been a problem, but he came with 10,000 of his disciples. He declared that they were very hungry and expected the Pandavas to feed them. How does one arrange to feed 10,001 people without advance notice? How does one arrange to feed 10,001 people in a forest, even with advance notice?

To buy some time to think of a way out, Yudhishthira asked the sage and his students to freshen up at a nearby river. He told them that when they returned, they would have meals ready to serve them. While the Pandava brothers panicked, Draupadi did what she always did in trouble—remembered her friend Krishna. Surprisingly, as soon as she remembered him, he appeared at her doorstep. It was as if there was some invisible cord binding their hearts, and Krishna already knew that she would be needing his help. Instead of helping her, Krishna told her that he too was hungry. Now Draupadi was at her wit's end. There were already 10,001 hungry men waiting to be fed, and now her friend had added his name to the list. She wasn't feeling so bad about not being able to feed the others as about not being able to feed the hungry Krishna. With an enigmatic smile, Krishna told her to bring her magical vessel. Draupadi had been gifted a magical vessel by Surya, the sun god. This vessel could feed an unlimited number of people unlimited quantities of food every day. Then what was the problem, you might ask. The problem was that once Draupadi had eaten her meal and washed the vessel, it would stop working till the next sunrise. Durvasa and his students had arrived when she had already eaten and washed the vessel.

Not knowing why Krishna was asking her for it, she handed the washed vessel to him. He carefully looked at it from all directions, turning it over and over. He found a single grain of rice stuck to it which Draupadi had not washed away. Krishna picked up that grain and dropped it into his mouth. As soon as Krishna ate that single grain of rice, all the 10,001 men at the riverside began to belch. Mysteriously, each of them felt full. Not wanting to embarrass themselves by refusing to eat at the house of the virtuous Pandavas, the sage and his students left. Draupadi couldn't discern what her friend had done to help her, but she understood all her problems were resolved when he was present. Not even her closest family offered her the kind of support she got from Krishna. Krishna was present not just during her troubles, but even in the good times. Not a single joyful event in the lives of the Pandavas passed without Krishna's presence. He made himself available in spite of his busy lifestyle.

With a Krishna by our side, we can keep walking, keep on carrying the weight of troubles that previously seemed unbearable. But humans, it seems, naturally love to beat each other at things. The most popular video games involve hitting or killing other players to score points. It is always competitive—getting ahead in life at the cost of the other person. At a fair I visited was a game that involved hitting a toy man with a tomato so that it fell into a pond and made a splash. And who was the winner? The one who hit the toy the most times. This was the most popular game at the fair and everyone was queuing to hit the toy man. The games we love reflect our real life mindset: in our efforts to emerge on top of the list of competitors, we forget our humanity. However, friendship truly begins with the honest admission, 'I am not invincible; I cannot deal with everything life throws at me alone. I need someone who can be available when I need him or her, and that's okay.' It is evidence of strength to admit that you require help to get by in life—the strength to risk admitting in front of a friend that you are vulnerable and that you need them; the risk of acknowledging that there is a void within each one of us that only true love and friendship can fill.

Of course, one shouldn't look at friends as psychologists to turn to in distress, or as service providers when in need; one shouldn't see the gift of friendship as a contract of some kind and feel entitled to their needs being met by the other person, especially not if it is at the friend's expense. A friend stands by you out of choice, with no expectation of anything in return; a true friend does not look at you as someone to compete with and beat in your most vulnerable hours. The knowledge that there is a friend who is waiting, willing, available at any hour, under any circumstances, is what makes friendship more important than blood relationships. Sharing means listening with your heart, supporting the other, being present and available.

People to whom the desire to help comes naturally, almost as a reflex, are those who have understood the importance of friendship. A friend is someone who tunes into people's needs and uses this knowledge not to outrun them, but to help them. Most of us are only in tune with our own needs. At the most, we might extend ourselves to accommodate the needs of our immediate families. Only a few tune in to the needs of their friends. What if helping another was not just something to be practised with family or friends? Imagine if helping people was a natural response. What a wonderful place the world would be! Did you know that those who help others also get helped most often? The universe conspires to return that help through some other agency, if not via the person whom you help. When you help someone, you don't just help them, you create a bond—visiting cards may be forgotten, but a visit to the heart is never forgotten.

Take the case of Sona and her friend Neil. They were in junior college, dreaming of a bright future. They spent many an hour discussing how they would go about their careers. Sona wanted to be a doctor and Neil a lawyer. Their talk centred on only these two professions whenever they met.

One day, Sona was surprised to find Neil sobbing in college.

'What's wrong?' she enquired fearfully, never having seen Neil cry before.

Neil was unable to speak. His words faltered, 'My father has suffered a huge business setback and he's facing bankruptcy. We have no money now! How will I pay for the law tuition fee and entrance exam? My future is ruined. My dreams are shattered.'

Sona was shattered too. She could feel his pain because she knew how much he wanted to be a lawyer. Not for a moment did she think that now she would be the only one to fulfil her dreams. This was their worst nightmare. Trying to think straight, she consoled Neil, 'Let's think of a way out. Let me ask my parents if they can pay for you.'

Neil gaped at her. He had not expected that kind of help from anyone. Even if her parents refused, he was grateful that at least she was trying to help him. He was not alone in this traumatic time. He wiped his tears and smiled at her. 'Thank you so much, Sona. I will always be grateful to you.'

That evening, Sona spoke to her parents, 'Mom, Dad, Neil is a great student. Could you pay his fee, please? His future is at stake here. Who else can he turn to? I so want to help him.'

Her parents were pleased by Sona's compassion for a friend in distress. They did not want to disappoint her and they readily agreed, grateful to God that they were in a position to help others. Sona was jubilant. She rushed to tell Neil the good news and they celebrated together by going out for their favourite ice creams.

Time flew by. Sona was now a surgeon and Neil a lawyer. Although still friends, they were busy in their professions. One day, however, Sona's world came crashing down. One of her high-profile patients had died on the operation table and his relatives had filed a suit against her for negligence. She knew she was innocent. She had done everything possible to save him and she could not be held responsible for his death. But the distressed relatives would hear none of this. Her name was tarnished by a legal battle and her reputation took a hit. She became depressed fearing the loss of her entire practice, which she had built up painstakingly with hard work and dedication.

Soon, the news reached Neil. He rushed to her side and asked to hear her side of the story. He spent many hours going over the details and finally said, 'Sona, I'm surprised you did not call me when this happened. I could have easily got you out of this mess. Leave everything to me now. I will send a legal reply to the relatives and talk to them, explaining that their case is very weak. If they still insist on fighting it out, I will be your lawyer. And let me assure you, I never lose a case.'

Sona hugged him with relief. Neil continued emotionally, 'Had it not been for your help, I would have never fulfilled my dreams. I owe you everything, Sona. I will get you out of this mess.'

True to his words, Neil fought for her and Sona was eventually found not guilty.

When Sona tried to thank him, he said, 'Oh hush! One good turn deserves another.'

She thanked her lucky stars and her parents for helping Neil when she asked. He had repaid her many times over. Sona had visited Neil's heart when he was in need and later Neil visited hers in adversity.

Now, if they had seen each other as competitors at the time they were both setting off to make their mark in the world, it was possible that neither would have fulfilled their dreams. But they chose to help each other instead. In fact, when you prioritize helping, will you see many more opportunities to do that. When you prioritize your own needs, you will see only objects to satisfy them. What you prioritize, you perceive. If you see only what is going on within you, you get opportunities only to seek help from others to fulfil your needs. But if you keep your eyes open to what is going on around you, you get plenty of opportunities to help others.

Generosity shouldn't be offered with strings attached, however. The purpose of generosity is satisfaction. There are many who have a lot but seldom give to others, mainly because they are trapped in the poverty mindset. On the other hand, there are many who have hardly anything but always give, because they are liberated by the magnanimity mindset.

The poverty mindset culminates in the law of subtraction; the magnanimity mindset culminates in the law of attraction. The law of subtraction states that when you give, you lose. The law of attraction states that when you give, you gain.

Do you believe in the laws of subtraction and attraction? Please read the following story before you decide: the old but true story of a famous Polish pianist of the late nineteenth-early twentieth century, Ignacy Jan Paderewski. There were four friends trying to raise money to fund their education. Their plan was to invite a famous pianist of their time, Ignacy Jan Paderewski, to perform a concert, give him a fee and then sell tickets to raise money. On paper, it seemed like a sound idea, but when they implemented it, they could not even raise enough to pay the pianist's fee. They gave him whatever money they had collected, which was $16,000, and were still short by $400. They not only owed him $400, they had nothing left to pay for their education either. However, the pianist was kind to them and returned the money, saying they should use it to pay for the expenses plus their college fee. He would take some money if any were left over.

After World War I, Ignacy Jan Paderewski rose to become the head of Poland. Hit by famine, Poland had nothing to feed its starving population. The pianist, now head of state, appealed to Herbert Hoover, in charge of the US Food and Relief Bureau. In response, Hoover sent thousands of tons of food to Poland, no questions asked. This was surprising conduct from an agency of its stature: to send relief without any kind of protocol. A grateful Paderewski went to meet Hoover to thank him for his timely help in an emergency. Hoover beamed at him and said, 'I only thanked you for what you did for me when I was in college.' No reward for guessing that Hoover was one of the four students who was benefitted by Paderewski's generosity. That's what generosity can sometimes achieve. The poverty mindset makes you poor in the heart and bankrupt in relationships. The magnanimity mindset makes you rich in the heart and richer in relationships.

When you interact with friends, you have two choices: you focus on either how much you can take or on how much you can give without worrying about what you receive in return. In his book *Give and Take*, Adam Grant talks about three types of people: takers, matchers and givers.

- ❖ Takers like to take more than they give.
- ❖ Givers are relatively rare and tilt in the opposite direction. They prefer to give more than they get. The takers help strategically and offer help only when the benefits outweigh the personal costs. The givers help whenever the benefits to other exceeds the personal costs.
- ❖ However, the third breed, the matchers, tries to achieve a balance between giving and getting. They believe in exchanging favours.

Who do you think are the most successful of the three? Takers, right? Absolutely wrong! According to the research mentioned by Adam Grant in his book, some of the most successful people were found to be givers. But that's not even the most interesting conclusion. The most interesting conclusion is that when takers succeed, someone usually loses. But when givers succeed, there is a ripple effect that causes all those around them to win too. There is a wealth of such research being conducted around the world about what makes the most successful people successful.

A pivotal question to ask before you become a giver is: do your friends simply change the routine of your life, or do they change the quality of your life? For a relationship to qualify as friendship, there has to be some depth in it. Just hanging out together doesn't make you friends. Playing together doesn't qualify as friendship either. A change of routine is definitely needed, no doubt. We need people around us who can play with us and have fun with us. We do need people who add colour to our lives, but we also need people who add value to our lives. There will be many around you to fulfil your entertainment needs. But there should be at least one who can make difficult moments in life fade into oblivion. True friends add joy to even the dullest parts of our life. True friends know how to lift our spirits. They know how to tell their stories and they know how to remember others' stories. Telling stories opens up the heart and remembering others' stories wins their hearts.

Don't we just love to speak about ourselves? Oh, we do! In most conversations, there is a subtle tug-of-war for attention. The moment we encounter someone willing to hear our story, our heart melts.

This is one level of engagement in which one listens to others tell their story, but remembering their story and recounting it later is the next level.

When you speak about others, it makes them feel important. Anyone who makes me feel important becomes important to me.

I will tell you how Shyam successfully used a personal touch in his relationships.

He was popular in college for being a good footballer. He was the star player in the football team and won many accolades for the college. His name was being considered for the captain of the team. Being the captain was a great honour. You could say that was his dream. But there was a teeny-weeny possibility that he might not be selected as captain because Chander was in the race too. One of the two was slated to be the next captain. The tide could turn either way. The final decision would be taken by the coach, and the coach had called them individually for meetings before taking the final call.

Shyam was in his office now. While they were talking, the coach was busy arranging his music CDs with loving care. Shyam recollected the advice the coach had given him last season: to listen to Raga Darbari and Raga Kedaram before a match to ease the tension. He brought up the subject again, saying, 'Coach, do you recall your suggestion last season to me? It worked wonders. Now I listen to these ragas to relax myself even before exams.'

The coach immediately came back to the table and sat down in front of him. 'That's wonderful, Shyam,' he said. Shyam felt the topic of the ragas had energized the coach. This encouraged Shyam to ask, 'Coach, how do you know so much about music?'

The coach was clearly enthusiastic about his favourite subject.

'You know, Shyam, music is therapy. It has the power to affect the subtle energies of the human body and lead to therapeutic changes. Take Raga Bhairavi. Did you know it can alleviate pain and anxiety in conditions ranging from toothache to cancer?"

---

* 'Music therapy to heal cancer patients', *Times of India*, 21 April 2016, https://timesofindia.indiatimes.com/life-style/health-fitness/de-stress/Music-therapy-to-heal-cancer-patients/articleshow/51921616.cms

'Oh really?' asked Shyam. 'Is it that powerful? Is that the secret of your success and health?'

'Music therapy is a branch of study by itself. I have studied the effect of music on the human brain and have presented papers on it. Yes, I do prefer to use this therapy in every way possible. But Shyam, this is my secret, I never tell anyone about it. Promise me that you will keep it to yourself.'

'Of course, coach,' Shyam promised. 'I hope to learn more from you about this wonderful science.'

The coach was delighted. Most people believed music therapy to be nothing but the placebo effect. At least Shyam had experienced its benefits first-hand. It was easy talking to those who did not think of it as hocus-pocus.

Soon, Chander arrived for his meeting and the coach became quiet again, reverting to the subject of football. Chander had no idea how animated he had been a few minutes back on the subject of music. Shyam got up to leave, but the coach asked him to stay. After he was done with Chander, he directed his attention back to Shyam and they discussed the nuances of music and football for a couple of hours. Finally, the coach said he would tell them his decision tomorrow.

The coach had no doubt who would be next captain: Shyam. He would rather pick someone who was in sync with his theories and beliefs. Together, they would make their team unbeatable. Shyam was not surprised to hear his decision. He knew he had struck the right chord with him the minute he had appreciated music.

Listening and appreciation are the two pillars of friendship. As Dale Carnegie put it, 'You can win more friends with your ears than you can with your mouth.'

Whose company you are in matters. Choose your company carefully. Your growth or decline depends on your choice. The *Niti Shataka* has a beautiful verse that puts it best.

santapyasi samstitasya payaso namapi na sruyate
muktakarataya tadeva nalinipatrasthitam drsyate
svatyam sagarasuktimadhyapatitam sanmauktikam jayate
prayemadhamamadhyamottamagunah samsargato jayate

(A drop of water falling on a hot iron pan disappears the instant it touches the hot metal. This is the outcome of keeping company with inferior minds. You cease to exist. When that same drop falls on the waxy surface of a lotus leaf, it shines like a pearl. This is the result of keeping company with mediocre minds. The person seems to be valuable to others, but is actually not. However, if that same drop falls into an oyster shell, it transforms into a shimmering pearl. The company of elevated minds results in mature individuals who are mature and can help others grow)

The quality of your friends determines the end result of your self-growth.

Summary:

- Friendship should not be about competition, it should be about helping each other grow.
- Be a giver, not just a taker. Give without expectations.
- However, choose who to give wisely. Your friendship should be deep and meaningful.

Activities

A. From the bandhus in your wheel of friendship, gauge who are givers, takers and matchers, competitors, cooperative.

Quality	Names
GIVERS	
TAKERS	
MATCHERS	
COMPETITORS	
COOPERATIVE	

B. Now that you have read till here, do you think differently about some of your friends? Place your friends again on the Wheel of Friendship to see if anything changes.

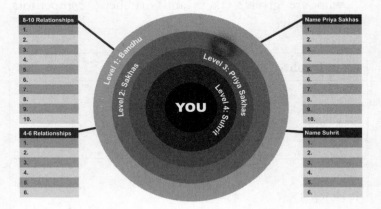

8-10 Relationships
1.
2.
3.
4.
5.
6.
7.
8.
9.
10.

4-6 Relationships
1.
2.
3.
4.
5.
6.

Level 1: Bandhu
Level 2: Sakhas
Level 3: Priya Sakhas
Level 4: Suhrit
YOU

Name Priya Sakhas
1.
2.
3.
4.
5.
6.
7.
8.
9.
10.

Name Suhrit
1.
2.
3.
4.
5.
6.

5

Peer Pressure and Self-Esteem

This chapter is dedicated to teenagers; however, whatever your age, you could be going through the same problems at the hands of your friends or colleagues.

A sure-shot formula for a life of misery is to allow others to determine your likes and dislikes. Being accepted by your friends is important. But is it necessary to strangle your own individuality?

Adolescence and teenage are periods to explore and discover oneself. There's a whole lot of confusion, too, with so many changes happening inside and outside the body simultaneously. Since one is still coming to terms with the new developments of body and mind, the confusion is compounded when one's relatives and friends offer their unsolicited opinions. These opinions, more often than not, eclipse one's own opinions because being accepted by our friends and others is the one single factor that determines happiness for many of us at that age.

This peer pressure is what shapes young minds for better or for worse. Peer pressure moulds most of the habits, both physical and mental, that people hold on to throughout their lifetimes. Just like a potter gives a shape to wet clay by putting pressure with his hands at certain points, peers shape the future of a young mind by applying pressure in different aspects of life. But unlike a potter, friends don't realize how their actions are moulding the futures of their friends. You might ask, why do we succumb to peer pressure so easily? There are many reasons why.

First and foremost is the fear of rejection. Who wants to be rejected? Especially when you are struggling to grapple with hormonal changes that erode your sense of normalcy. In fact, a young mind will go to any extent to avoid rejection, even to the extent of compromising on lifelong values and principles. Let us take the example of Bunty, aged seventeen, who had been a disciplined boy all through his school life. Naturally, his parents were shocked when they were called to the police station after being caught stealing a car for a joyride with his friends. He himself was distraught and puzzled about why he did that. He had no intention of doing anything to hurt his parents, let alone something illegal. But the minute he met his friends, his personality flipped and he was no longer in full control of his actions.

The second and probably the biggest fear a young mind has is to be made fun of. When strangers humiliate you, it doesn't hurt as much as when your own friends, the people you love, do; it's unbearable! Young minds are often willing to bend over backwards to avoid being made fun of. Peers can sometimes really hurt. Have you had this experience? If you have, you must know exactly how badly it hurts. Sometimes, when friends become a bit familiar with each other, they begin to take each other for granted. In such cases, humour might occasionally lead to sadistic pleasure. And often, friends end up bringing up something others are sensitive about, hurting one another immensely. Sharing light moments is a very important part of friendship—it is so important that you could even call it the trunk of friendship! But the downside is, when light moments take a darker turn and two friends end up pulling each other's leg out of spite till it hurts in the heart, it might sometimes destroy those friendships. And truly, these can be as hurtful (possibly even more) as break-ups in romantic relationships.

Lisa and Shekhar were to get married in a year's time. They had decided to wait till marriage to have sex. It was a decision based on their moral and cultural upbringing. But their friends were all sexually active and were urging them not to wait. Lisa and Shekhar didn't want to cave in, but at the same time, they didn't want to seem like the abnormal couple among their group of friends. At this point we're giving reasons for when and how people succumb to peer pressure; not discussing solutions. Different people would handle the situation differently depending on their value structure.

A third reason why one succumbs to peer pressure is the simple desire not to lose a friend. Friends are important. In some ways, life revolves around friendship. We might sometimes go to any extent to stay in the friends' circle. Imagine a scenario at a party. If a friend hands you a beer bottle, two voices immediately react from within you: one voice chastises and tells you you are a fool for accepting the bottle. At the same time, another voice comforts you, saying that you need to do this or you might lose this friend. In other words, it justifies your impulse to neglect your individual likes and dislikes for the sake of maintaining your group dynamics and friendship needs.

Ami was back from a holiday in Switzerland. Although her parents could ill afford an extravagant vacation, Ami had insisted, cried and threatened them till they agreed. All her friends went abroad in summer holidays and she did not want to be the odd one out. Not that she didn't know her parents' financial status—it was just too important for her to be part of the group she called her friends. Her parents wondered what would happen next year when they could not take her to any foreign destination. They decided she needed counselling to stop buckling under peer pressure. The counsellor helped her understand that friendship depends not on where her family goes on vacation but how she is as a person. Being helpful, caring, kind, honest, all such qualities would attract her friends more than flaunting her holiday destination. Genuine people are rare and if one is genuinely not embarrassed about one's social status, others too find it to be an insignificant part in friendship. The counsellor also discussed the issue of FOMO—fear of missing out. This fear propels teenagers to do insane things. Ami understood that her anxiety of missing out on similar experiences as her friends had no end to it and the sooner she overcame it the better it would be for all concerned.

Softer guys may turn into followers of their friends because they do not want to hurt their feelings. But in the bargain, they bury their own hurt. They are too worried about what others might say and think it better to undermine their own feelings. This continues infinitely till one day, the bag of suppressed emotions explodes and puts an end to the friendship. Look at what happened to Harish. Harish had never had any interest in clothes. But all of a sudden, he began demanding money from his parents to buy branded clothes. For the first few times, his parents let him, assuming it was a phase that would soon pass. But when his demands continued, they spotted a problem. When they refused to indulge his desire, he threw a terrible tantrum, bringing the house down. The parents were dumbfounded, not knowing what had come over their gentle boy. He didn't even dress in this way. Why then did he insist on buying these clothes? One day, they sat him down and asked him gently what was making him buy those clothes. Harish sadly explained to them that his best friend had formed a club where members had to wear only branded clothes. He did not even want to join the club but his friend said he would be very unhappy if he did not join. He was buying and wearing those clothes only for the sake of his friend's happiness!

Yet another reason that youngsters yield to peer pressure may be that they want to convince themselves and the big bad world looking down at them that they have now grown up and can make their own big decisions. Just to prove this point, they end up taking bad decisions and harming themselves.

Look at how Shashi dealt with peer pressure in his school. Shashi was the only boy in his class who was not interested in watching porn. His classmates mocked him for having a 'holier than thou' attitude, but he didn't care. He did not want to be one of the boys, so he made friends in his literary club and bird-watching club, who shared his interests. His schooldays were not entirely happy, but it was better than being forced by peer pressure to do what he had no interest in. Shashi could handle the peer pressure positively, not giving in to his friends' insistence that he watch porn with them.

External stability is often mistaken for being in control internally. This means that when people control others they feel they are in control of themselves and therefore feel confident. Being in control of oneself is not easy. In fact, it is what most spiritual practices aim for. Controlling others is much easier and may even be the main cause behind bullying. Let me tell you the story of Hardik. Hardik was standing for class representative in the college elections. He expected his friends to vote for him. But to his surprise, they said that they would only vote for him if he proved he had the power to control the juniors. Instead of ignoring their comments, Hardik decided to take up the challenge. He called the juniors and ragged them in front of his friends. However, the principal learnt of this and Hardik was suspended from college. He ended up losing even what he had.

At this point, I would like you to ask yourself two questions:

1. Are you aware of what makes you unique?
2. Do you have a healthy self-image?

Lack of awareness of your strengths and an unhealthy self-image are the primary causes behind succumbing to peer pressure. People who succumb to peer pressure are often pretending to be someone else. Those who give in to bullies are forced to be someone else. Either way, it is their individuality that is compromised. It sets up a chain of toxic events: when you doubt yourself, you hate yourself. And when you hate yourself, you proclaim enmity with yourself. Enmity with self extends to enmity with others. You slowly begin to feel inferior to everyone else, convinced that everyone is out to get you. Then comes a stage when even a smile looks like it hides a threat. Remember, abilities and talents do not necessarily make one worthwhile.

A person with a weak self-image develops that image based on others' perception of them. However, it has more to do with how we think we appear to others. That is, based on our perceptions of others, we imagine what their judgement would be and this becomes the foundation of our self-judgement. In essence, the image we have of ourselves is a combination of our imagination and others' perceptions. The most basic human needs are food, clothing, shelter, etc., but our need for safety and security, love and emotional support, dignity and self-esteem is equally important.

Self-esteem refers to the way we look at ourselves, which, in turn, affects everything we do in our life. Our self-esteem determines our success and failure in every walk of life, from our careers to our relationships. The decisions and choices we make are heavily influenced by our self-esteem. Self-esteem is, essentially, the combination of self-confidence, which is confidence in one's abilities, and self-respect, which is a feeling of worthiness. Your ability to understand and deal with challenges has a direct relationship with your self-confidence. Your ability to stand up to protect your interests, needs and happiness is determined by the respect you have for yourself and your interests—your self-respect. Here are a few questions to ask yourself if you are unsure about what your self-esteem levels are like:

1. Have you wondered how some people are so good at speaking or performing on stage and compared yourself to them?
2. Have you ever felt inadequate when you observed their confident smiles and wondered where it was all coming from?
3. Do you struggle to start a conversation with a person you want to talk to?
4. Do you ever feel like you are a total waste of flesh and bones and do not fit into a social group of dynamic individuals?
5. Have you ever felt helpless and thought that you were useless because you were unable to do something you always aspired to do?

6. Do you relate less to the people who stand up to the challenge when times get tough than those who crouch low and attempt to be invisible in the face of adversity?

If you answered 'yes' to more than one of these questions, you might have low self-esteem even if you have never felt like it before. Those who have high self-esteem are confident about their competence in relation to the people around them and feel worthy of respect. They are more resilient, better equipped to deal with challenges and resist peer pressure out of respect for the morals they choose and the things they believe in.

Those who have low self-esteem feel incompetent, unworthy and like misfits in society. They feel they are totally wasted as people, unworthy of achieving anything or proving themselves. And this is yet another important factor that causes people to give in to peer pressure: confusion. Peers end up putting unwarranted pressure on one another to do some things that they feel unsure about doing alone during the years when they are struggling to find their identities. It may often culminate in sticky situations in which none of the peers know how to handle the consequence of their actions and are sometimes left with no way out.

Sana, aged fifteen, got together with her friends to secretly flick a pistol one of their fathers had. Knowing very well the dangers of firearms, it seemed like an irresistible idea. They went to a remote part of their estate and fiddled with the gun. Loading it, they aimed a few shots at the birds on the tree. Excitedly, they all grabbed the pistol from one hand to another and before they knew it, a shot was fired at a friend. She was grievously injured and was hospitalized for many days. Sana alone would never have dared to touch a gun, knowing its dangers full well, but in the company of friends, the adventure index overtook the danger index.

Let me share with you an interesting study conducted by the National Institute on Drug Abuse (NIDA)[*] on teens in 2012. In order to find out why teens succumb to peer pressure so often, they conducted a study on how teens perceive risks and rewards that are connected to their decisions. In this connection, they monitored the brain activities of teens who drove motor vehicles. Their studies revealed that when teens drove with friends in their car, they were more likely to take risks than when driving alone. Studies also revealed that teens were more likely to take risks when their friends were in the car than when adults were in the car in the same situation. They concluded that teens focused only on actions that their friends considered cool. They didn't care how much risk was involved in that action. They simply cherished being rewarded with appreciative comments or some sort of acknowledgement of how cool they were. When they were with adults, they are constantly aware of risks and thus drive carefully. But when they were with friends, the focus shifts to the rewards, not on the risks involved.

---

[*] 'Why Does Peer Pressure Influence Teens To Try Drugs?' National Institute for Drug Abuse for Teens, https:// teens.drugabuse.gov/blog/post/why-does-peer-pressure-influence-teens-try-drugs

Let's go back to the topic of bullying. The way to look at bullying is simple. Being bullied is not the only problem—the bully has a problem too. Let me explain this. Bullies are actually not as strong as they appear to be. In fact, they may have a weakness, because of which bullying others helps them feel better about themselves. Evoking fear in the eyes of another person might actually be giving them a sense of control and accomplishment that they lack. The more fear you show, the more powerful they feel. This is how a bully's mind justifies and rationalizes the inhuman act of undermining a person's self-worth. Bullies might want just entertainment or they might want you to do things for them; they come in every size, gender, occupation and even relationship. I know of teens who are severely bullied by their parents. There are others whose siblings bully them. Yet others have friends who bully them. Even your boss at work or professor in a university could be a bully. In fact, strangers can be bullies too; someone who doesn't know you at all and someone you haven't even seen before is most likely to bully you. A medium enabling bullying today is social media, where people hide behind screens to try to influence your opinions, likes and dislikes, often unkindly. Whether it's done by strangers or by people whom you know intimately, bullying is probably one of the worst experiences for a young person.

We see that teens get bullied for the most trivial reasons. One girl was bullied for having a name that was more appropriate for boys. When friends bullied youngsters like Simi, she believed that's how friends behaved. It was a price she was willing to pay to be a part of her friends' circle, never realizing that she was being bullied. Only when she changed schools did she realize that friendship is about companionship. But sometimes, bullying can take sinister forms. Take the example of Priya. Priya was a short but a nimble gymnast. Maybe her success provoked taller girls to bully her. They manhandled her whenever they could and being small, she could never retaliate. One day, she was standing at the edge of the school swimming pool, waiting for the coach to arrive, when she felt a pair of hands grab her ankles and shove her into the pool. She wasn't a good swimmer and nearly drowned as she struggled to come to the surface and reach the edge. But she was again pushed in by more hands and kept underwater for so long that when they finally let go, she couldn't hear and couldn't think. When the coach asked her why she went into the pool, she couldn't answer him. Even today, no one knows that she nearly died from being bullied. And even today, Priya is afraid of entering a swimming pool.

Here's another heart-wrenching story of bullying that nearly ended in a tragedy. Diya was tall and thin. At twelve, she towered over all her classmates, both girls and boys. They called her 'Eiffel Tower', laughed at her, poked fun at her height and excluded her from all their activities. She was left alone. Whoever tried to be her friend was threatened as well and so no one befriended her. Her parents tried to invite some classmates home but they all refused to come for fear of being bullied if they were seen with her. Her parents tried to explain to her the advantages of being tall and how it was an asset for her but her young mind could not understand whether her parents were right or her so-called friends. Feeling lonely and miserable, she came down with a stomach infection, helicobacter pylori. The infection took a toll on her health, leaving her weak and thin. Her parents took her out of school and tried home schooling. But she was so deeply depressed that she lost her appetite. She would go for days without eating and resist every attempt to be fed. She was diagnosed with anorexia nervosa, in which a person refuses to eat for fear of gaining weight. The cause was certainly psychological. The bullying experiences had been too traumatic and her brain was unable to cope with the trauma. Her anorexia reached a point where if she was forced to eat, she would go and vomit it all out. She lost weight and was getting progressively more malnourished. Their doctor advised her to be hospitalized or her body would shut down due to lack of nutrition. She slowly recovered physically, but mentally, she never did.

Bullies prey on perceived weakness, insecurity or sensitivity. But wait a minute! Is there anyone in this world who doesn't have any weakness or insecurity? Absolutely no one. Which means everyone is vulnerable to being bullied. Human beings are flawed and full of limitations. Bullies can hurt only those who don't know themselves or are confused about themselves. Bullies try to define you and do so in a way that hurts you and demeans you; in a way that you lose confidence in yourself. But bullies can cause hurt only to those who haven't discovered themselves yet. A bully cannot define those who have already defined themselves clearly in their mind. When you refuse to give a bully the power to control you or make you feel bad, they cannot do anything to you. The secret is to take responsibility for your own happiness. We cannot allow others to decide what brings us happiness. People may pick on you for all your shortcomings, but it is your inner strength which will prevent them from truly affecting you. More than anything else, your family and friends are the ones who help you find your strength and stand behind you no matter what. The moment you seek out your inner strength and the external support of people who love you unconditionally, no bully can truly exercise control over you. Everybody oscillates between these two extremes: sometimes, they feel confident and sometimes, they feel stupid; sometimes they feel worthy and sometimes, unworthy. Sometimes, you love yourself and at other times, you hate yourself. And it is in the times when you are weak and don't feel great about yourself that your friends and family remind you that you are worthy and loveable.

Dealing with Insecurities

Vicky, a law intern, preferred spending long hours at the office. While most interns cribbed about spending their entire lives in the office, Vicky felt thankful. 'It gives me an opportunity to avoid having any relationships,' he admitted quite candidly, 'because it's difficult for me to give and take love.' On prodding further, he said, 'Deep inside, a voice tells me that I'm not loveable—nothing within me is worth loving. I have no extraordinary qualities that would attract other people to me. So I try to find solace in my work and not look to people for comfort.'

Similarly, Gita was an exceptional student. Always a topper. Her attempt at suicide, thus, came as a shock to her family and friends. Why would an achiever be so dissatisfied with life? Here's what she had to say, 'I worked harder than everyone else to prove to myself that I was not less than anyone. Because everyone in my family is a doctor, as a child, I was constantly asked if I would continue the family tradition. I asked myself if I was good enough. I was always made to feel that maybe I was not eligible to be a part of my family unless I became a doctor. This goaded me to put in extra effort to prove my worthiness, even if it killed me. But after college, I couldn't go on like that. The anxiety of not being on top was killing me. Rather than see academic failure and be rejected by family, it made more sense to get out of the scene. Suicide seemed like the best option to save myself the misery of living through disappointment.' Of course, after she went through therapy, Gita got insights that helped her deal with her insecurities. She realized that her family loved her irrespective of what profession she chose to be in and that she did not have to prove her merit at every step. Life was not one long exam that had to be topped but a book of wisdom to get insights from.

Chirag was the class joker. He made everyone laugh with his silly behaviour. But that was only an act. Buried within that joker was a fearful teenager, a teenager afraid of losing if he competed with his peers. 'I feel that my classmates were way ahead of me in knowledge, talent and whatever it took to be successful. I don't have that something necessary for success. Something is wrong with me but I can't put a finger on it. What I know is that I'm a loser, so I cover it up by being a joker who makes people laugh and hence, nothing great is expected of him.' During counselling, he was asked to focus on his strengths, work on his own expectations and not draw comparisons. Once he began to see how he was demeaning himself and being self-destructive, there was a sea change in his personality and he could put away the joker persona he always wore.

When good things happen, the natural reaction is joy. But when good things happened to Vinay, his normal reaction was disbelief. Every time he cleared an exam, an interview, got a job, he would think, 'Wait, there must be a mistake somewhere, this couldn't be happening to me.' He kept anticipating that the wall would collapse on him if he allowed himself to be happy, and soon, he took to drinking to ease his anxiety. After a few drinks, he would become numb and have no anxiety about all that was good in his life. No fear of everything falling apart. It made him feel in control. His counsellor said that it might benefit him to recognize that this was his defence mechanism for an underlying, repressed feeling that he was undeserving of anything good. Subconsciously, he felt unworthy of any happiness, so he made sure he did not accept any happiness that came his way, to the extent that he would sabotage his real life to prove that his subconscious diktat was right.

Low self-esteem develops primarily due to two reasons: one is because of others, who look down on us and keep giving us negative inputs and second, because we look down on ourselves and keep beating ourselves up for our mistakes or shortcomings. Others may be looking down on us out of meanness or their own insecurities, but we look down on ourselves because we judge ourselves without compassion.

The number of people who are actually mean is much lower than the number of people who are insecure. Insecurity again stems from low self-esteem. That means people who have low self-esteem tend to look down on others and use the negativity they feel towards themselves to bring down other people's self-esteem so they feel superior to them.

The favourite strategy of a bully is to identify and focus on something unique about their target. Once they identify that, the next step is to create a sense of insecurity in their target about that uniqueness. Once that insecurity is established irrevocably in the target's mind, the bully goes on to cause hurt, emotionally at first, and in worst-case scenarios, physically. Once that's done, the bully simply steps out and allows the target to self-harm. When the target internalizes the hurt caused by the bully and begins to believe it, the process of self-bullying begins. The target begins to blame and criticize himself. Finally, the target tries to change or hide the uniqueness in order to prevent further bullying. When you become ashamed of your uniqueness, the bully can claim his ultimate victory.

Seema was so pretty that if you looked at her once, you would surely look again. It was not surprising that people complimented her all the time. However, her own friends became hostile towards her after she won a beauty pageant at school and started picking on her. They called her 'bird brain' because of the popular belief that those who are beautiful cannot be brainy! She was one of the intelligent students in her class, yet, they insulted her. Some of them would even say, 'You are stupid and annoying. I hate you and so does everyone else.' And when she cried, they turned even nastier. They would throw ink on her dress and then laugh at her. When she tried to run from them, they would trip her. No one bothered to help her. She would go home all black and blue and wanting to kill herself. It reached a point where she actually began to believe that she was brainless. Her academic performance deteriorated and she flunked the ninth grade. Her self-esteem was at its lowest and she began to believe she could not continue with her education. If only somebody could've told her, 'Your uniqueness is your gift. When you reject your uniqueness, you reject yourself. Each one of us has been given unique gifts by our creator. Exploring that uniqueness and using it to our best capacity to serve society is the purpose of humanity.' By the time we actually identify our uniqueness, our childhood is past. By the time we begin to hone our uniqueness, our adolescence would, most likely, have passed too. Think about this: how can we allow one bully to come into our life and destroy the possibilities of exploring and growing with a few sadistic comments?

If you study nature carefully, there is no repetition. No two zebras have the same stripe patterns, no two bats emit sounds of the same frequency, no two butterflies have the exact same design on their wings, and no two humans' fingerprints are ever alike. That being the case, the only thing we really have in common as natural beings is that we all have unique traits. No matter what our defects and imperfections might seem to be, there is always something in us that is unique. Though we may not be proud of our defects and may even be displeased with them, there is always something in us that we are proud of. The objective of our lives is to find these things and use them for the greater good.

Self-acceptance is key. Self-acceptance is accepting yourself completely and wholeheartedly—accepting your shortcomings as well as your unique strengths. Once you have accepted yourself, you will be at peace with yourself. When you are at peace with yourself, your self-confidence and self-respect levels will automatically rise. When you are at peace internally, you will be inspired to create change to bring about peace in the world around you as well. The unwillingness to accept one's realities is the greatest cause of unhappiness.

Now let us take this discussion to the next level. So far, I have been focusing on you as an individual. Now let us apply this to friendship. When we do that, we will come across one of the greatest mistakes we make in our friendships and simultaneously, we will also find one of the greatest strengths of friendship. Just like we have our uniqueness, others have theirs too. When we can and should accept our uniqueness, why can't we accept the uniqueness of others? Like I said before, acceptance brings peace and non-acceptance brings negativity.

The moment you accept uniqueness, you accept people's differences. Unfortunately, friends often try to push one another to become more and more alike, thereby eliminating difference. At the beginning of this book, we spoke about like-mindedness being one of the crucial elements of friendship. Is there a difference between being like-minded and being alike? Yes, there is a vast difference!

When you force each other to be alike, it means that you are subtly trying to kill the uniqueness in each other. This is also a form of bullying. It is based on an incorrect belief that friendship means a relationship between two people who are identical, and that it is essential to force your friend to sacrifice their likes and dislikes to be just like you. Just like a photocopy machine makes copies of the original document, such people feel friendship is a machine to make people exact replicas of one another in every aspect. In forcing another to be like them or forcing others to make sacrifices of their interests for friendship, they are strangling the very essence of friendship, which lies in respecting each other's differences and not being in denial of them. But people often expect and force uniformity in friendships, which is totally unnatural and hence, unsustainable. This forced likeness strangles friendship.

Let me tell you the story of a deep friendship that was destroyed by a lack of respect for differences and artificially forcing the other to make sacrifices. This story is also from the Mahabharata. There were two best friends in a gurukul. They loved each other dearly and couldn't spend a moment without each other's company. Their gurukul years passed rapidly in each other's company and soon, it was time for them to part ways. One day, the two friends sat together, holding hands for the last time. From the next day onwards, their lives were going to be very different.

One was born into the royal family and was the heir to the kingdom's throne. The other was born in a poor Brahmin family and was to live a life of poverty, absorbed in higher contemplation. The prince was Drupada and the Brahmin was Drona. Drupada promised his friend that he would share his world with him.

But soon, life took them in completely different directions and they lost touch with each other for almost a decade. Drupada had become the king of the land by then while Drona became a teacher with a meagre income. When Drona's son was born and he was struggling to make ends meet, his wife prodded him to find a decent income. That's when Drona decided to encash his friendship with Drupada. He walked into the Drupada's courtroom without asking his permission and repeated to him his childhood promise, demanding that he be given half the kingdom. Drupada was shocked at such a claim. What he had committed in his childhood was out of love. But he could see that there was no longer any love in this friendship. Drupada immediately decided that this friendship wasn't worth it. How could a friend force another to give away half his property, wealth and rights? It was different if Drupada voluntarily gave it away to his friend. But at this point, it was simply a forceful claim. Drona thought that he and Drupada were equal just because they were friends and that equality should be established in every way. Either Drupada had to downgrade to Drona's level or he had to upgrade Drona to his level. Drona had grown up physically, but was still a child as far as his understanding of friendship was concerned.

Drupada refused. In fact, he even denied any friendship between them. Drona was shocked at that. How could he deny their friendship? Drupada's denial was not based on facts but on feelings. Friendship is not a legally binding contract that both parties have to stand by. Friendship is a heartfelt relationship into which people enter and stay in voluntarily. For a friendship to last a lifetime, both parties concerned have to invest in the relationship selflessly and with no expectations. Friendship thrives when there is like-mindedness. Like-minded friends need not be alike in their lifestyles and interests. In childhood, when they were friends, Drona and Drupada were like-minded and that is why their differences of lifestyle didn't matter and didn't impede their relationship. After a long gap in their relationship, ideally, Drona should have taken the time to re-establish the love they had for each other and reconnect on that level instead of demanding material benefits.

If you remember, we had also discussed the friendship of Krishna and Sudama earlier, who were also from different socio-economic backgrounds and had been childhood friends who reunited after a long time. But unlike Drona, Sudama first re-established their connection. He did not straightaway walk into Dwarka and demand something from Krishna in the name of their old friendship. He didn't force Krishna to give up his wealth and kingdom to become like him, neither did he force Krishna to elevate his social status by giving him half the kingdom. He simply expressed his love by offering him a small gift that was worthless from the monetary point of view. Sudama knew something that

Drona did not. Friendship cannot be forced; it has to be won. Friends shouldn't be expected to make sacrifices they don't want to. Everything in friendship is by choice.

Drona lost his friend because he demanded sacrifices. Drona lost his friend because he forced Drupad to give up his interests and focus on his own interests instead. Drona lost his friend because he tried to force his friend to eliminate their differences artificially.

People are different in many ways. Differences cannot be artificially or forcefully eliminated. What we are terming 'differences' from our point of view may actually be uniqueness from another perspective. Everybody responds differently to differences. Some people reject those who are different from them. This may take many forms, from racism to casteism, from classism to chauvinism. These people would want anyone seeking a relationship with them to first fit into their mould. The mould is fixed, rigid and designed to protect their interests. Anyone not ready to comply is rejected.

Some other people choose to 'tolerate' those that are different from them. They believe, 'I may not be able to appreciate the differences but at least I am ready to tolerate them for the sake of friendship.' When we say 'I tolerate', what we really mean to say is that we are superior. We may not be rejecting them for being different, but 'tolerance' doesn't mean the same thing as 'acceptance'. However, when you simply tolerate, there is no question of love. Of course, it is better than outright rejection of difference. When you tolerate another person's uniqueness, you at least give that person a chance to live life based on their terms because it allows them to remain happy, even if you don't like it.

Some other people *accept* those who are different from them. Accepting people as they are means more than simply tolerating their difference. When we accept people, we respect them: accepting their uniqueness is respecting their uniqueness. Those who accept us as we are ask for no explanations, pass no judgements, make no sarcastic comments to make us feel bad about our difference and no noxious remarks about these traits to other people either. Even if we dress differently, talk differently and live differently, it is all acceptable because we love each other. We take no notice of these superficial differences.

Acceptance of difference leaves room for both parties to grow. With acceptance come many opportunities for transformation. Acceptance breaks barriers between friends and acts as the life force of their friendship. It does not try to force a person into a mould or to do something they would rather not do. Instead, it is a warm, welcome embrace. It offers the friend a safe space to explore what they want to be. When we celebrate differences, we do something even greater: we celebrate uniqueness. Isn't it a top-of-the-world feeling to be supported and appreciated for your uniqueness? This is how friends bring out the best in us.

Like Anna Letitia Barbauld, a prominent English poet and author of children's literature, says, 'Friends should consider themselves as the sacred guardians of each other's virtues.'

Such friends provide the warmth of family outside our home. They create a place where we feel welcome, not threatened—they are like mothers who nurture us. Friendships like that can be life-changing, like the friendship of Rishi and Veda.

Veda was limping in school one day. His friends were alarmed. Had he hurt himself? Was he in pain?

'Oh no, my shoes are torn. The sole is going to fall off,' laughed Veda.

'Then why don't you go to the cobbler sitting outside?' his classmates suggested.

During the break, Veda limped to the cobbler. The cobbler had a son who would help his father mend shoes. Veda looked at the boy, his peer, and said, 'Rishi, why don't you come to school?'

Rishi was a friendly boy and Veda always liked to talk to him. That day, it struck Veda that Rishi should be in school, just like him. But Rishi was too poor to afford any education. After school, Veda went to play with Rishi. The cobbler asked him not to play with Rishi because he was rich and his parents might not like it. But Veda said he could play with anyone he liked. It never bothered him that his friend was poor, as long as they liked each other. Every day, when he went home, he had only one thought. How could he help his friend Rishi get an education?

After mulling over it for a couple of days, he spoke to his mother. 'Mom, Rishi, my friend, is a poor boy and he doesn't go to school. Do you think we could call him home in the evenings and you could teach him?' His mom was surprised at the suggestion. She spoke to his father and together, they thought they should set an example before Veda by helping the less privileged in any way they could.

Besides, Rishi and Veda were friends and friendship should be about encouraging each other. Veda was thrilled to know that his parents would help him help his friend and that Rishi would finally get a basic education. That's what friends are for. He went and told Rishi. The best reward for him was when Rishi shed tears of joy; he hugged Veda tightly to express his gratitude. Veda had not just decided to nurture Rishi through a school education, but had also understood that it was important to accept, celebrate and use their differences to benefit each other.

Friendship begins with acceptance and thrives if it is celebrated. Each of us is like a piece in the mega jigsaw puzzle of the Universe. Our strengths are the curves and our shortcomings are the slots in the pieces. Acceptance of the perfection of God's plans helps us handle our strengths with gratitude and weaknesses with humility. For every strength we have, there is a slot that has to be filled and for every weakness we have, there is a piece with the right curve to help us fill that void. When everyone acts in reverence for the plans of God and in accordance with the strengths and weaknesses assigned to us, a complete picture of God's plan emerges. The role of an orchestra conductor is to ensure the perfect symphony. To do that, he may have to occasionally silence the best of players for a few seconds. He knows that even silence enhances music. God may occasionally withhold a quality we hanker for. At such times, remember, God is the expert orchestra conductor; even our lack of that quality is a contribution to the Lord's plan.

We cannot achieve much alone. God always surrounds you with people who can help you with your weaknesses throughout your life. In return, you are expected to be available to someone else to help with his or her weaknesses. That's only fair, right? When my uniqueness complements yours, we will make a good pair. Friendship begins with the acceptance that I need you so I can learn from you what I need to become the person I aspire to be. Accepting it is one thing, but acknowledging that need verbally is another thing. It takes a great deal of humility to tell another that you need them. Try it for yourself and see. When you tell someone that you need them, for a moment, their feeling of self-worth skyrockets. People will do anything for someone who helps them experience a greater sense of self-worth. It gives us a great feeling to know that we have added value to another's life. It gets even better when someone verbally acknowledges our contribution to their lives.

Recognizing and acknowledging the need for another person in your life is not a sign of weakness, but of strength. Insecure people cannot and will not acknowledge that they need others to succeed in life. Secure people readily and happily admit that they need people around them to succeed.

When Vikram lost his life in a car accident, they recovered an old, worn-out piece of paper from his pocket. That paper meant a lot to him. It had a history. In school, his class was asked to write the name of every child in class and mention the best thing they could think of about every classmate. The teacher collected all the sheets and compiled what everyone had written. She made separate sheets with the name of the student on top and everything that was written for them by other children. The next day she handed each child the list with every good thing that was said about them. The class excitedly read about their good attributes and exploded with joy. Some felt more confident and some others basked in the pride. For some, it was a revelation to learn about their good qualities and for some, it was a validation of their self-belief. No one discussed this activity after that, till the class gathered again for Vikram's funeral years later.

His parents asked the teacher present if she recognized that paper. It was the paper that listed everything good his friends had said about him. He treasured it so much that he always kept it with him. They thanked her profusely for giving the kids so much love and attention. And then his best friend, Nicky, showed them all his own wallet and his list, saying that he, too, treasured it and had always kept it in his pocket. One by one, all his friends admitted that they had all saved that paper till date.

'It's in my diary.'

'It's framed in my room.'

'It's kept safely in a box.'

They had all kept it all those years—that was how precious it was to them!

The teacher cried at how a simple activity had meant so much. In a world that has no time for anyone, a few words of appreciation are cherished forever. The famous American author, Mark Twain, once wrote, 'I can live for two months on a good compliment.' Whenever you get an opportunity to compliment someone publicly, I would suggest you not let it go! According to a study in social science, when people are complimented, their performance and skills appear enhanced. In fact, it has been seen that some brain areas that enhance learning are activated when you are complimented.

When you make another person feel important, you gain a friend for life. A few words of appreciation go a long way in shaping somebody's life. This is not a tactic to win hearts, but a habit that will help you retain the hearts you win. Lives can be changed with a little appreciation.

When I was in school, I wasn't really able to do well in my studies, neither was I good at sports. Most teachers would pick on me negatively—at worst, they would find some reason to chastise me and at best, ignore me as if I didn't exist. This was the scenario for most of my schooldays till I got to the eighth grade. I had the option of choosing a third language and I chose French. I think that was one of the best choices I made; not only because I excelled at French, but because of the teacher who taught me. She was an old lady who was very strict. Everyone in school always made fun of her, though, of course, behind her back. No one dared to speak when she was in class. Somehow, she found something good in me. I must thank her for being the first teacher to find something valuable in me, and though numerous teachers have come and gone in my life, I still remember her because of all the appreciation and encouragement she gave me. The result of the attention I got from her was that I began to excel in all other subjects too. Soon, I was topping the class and eventually, the college I graduated from. Her words of appreciation and encouragement became the launch pad from which my life took off. While the entire school made fun of her, I silently admired her, because I believe that finding the good in people is an art.

There may be many differences between our friends and us. But that doesn't mean that I cannot find reasons to appreciate the good in the other person. Friendship thrives in spite of our differences in interests. That happens in the wake of genuine, heartfelt and appreciative words. When we practise celebrating differences through words of appreciation, our friendships grow.

Human beings are like an opal stone. Have you heard of the opal? Let me tell you a story about how Renu discovered a beautiful quality in the opal stone. Her love for exquisite diamond jewellery regularly took Renu to various diamond showrooms. She would spend hours admiring the shimmering stones studded in wonderful designs. One day, her eyes landed on a pale stone that seemed to be the odd one out among the glittering diamonds that surrounded it.

Her curiosity got the better of her and she called the jeweller to ask him about the stone. Why would he keep a pale stone among all the costly and shiny ones? He smiled at her, pulled out the pale stone and held it in the open palm of his left hand. He told her, 'This is an opal. Do you know what the other name of the opal is?' She shook her head. 'It's called the sensitive jewel,' he said. That caught her attention. He explained that the speciality of the opal became visible when it encountered warmth. Saying so, he cupped his left palm with his right palm, thus enclosing the opal within his hands for some time. After a minute, he opened his palm. To Renu's surprise, the formerly pale stone was now shimmering like a diamond. She was shocked to see the transformation. She couldn't believe that such wonders existed in nature.

Humans beings are also like opals: they are sensitive jewels. When people who seem unremarkable and unimpressive are given enough warmth, love, encouragement and appreciation, their good qualities begin to show. I encourage you to try this with your friends and see them transform. Add warmth to all your relationships and fill your friends' lives with words of encouragement and appreciation.

Summary:

- The more one succumbs to peer pressure, the more one is rejecting his self-worth.
- Friends are so important that one is willing to go against one's own likes and dislikes, undergoing all trials and tribulations to remain a link in the friendship chain.
- Self-doubt and self-hatred set you up for peer pressure; inner strength or outer support from family or adults offsets peer pressure.
- Acceptance of self and others paves the way for healthy friendships.

Activity

Create a list of people who are not on your Wheel of Friendship; they may be people you dislike or you rarely meet. Think and write one positive quality about that person.

Person	One positive quality about them

Now that you see something positive in these people, would you want to include any of them in your Wheel of Friendship?

6

Creating Value in Friendship

Ye kechid duhkhita loke sarve te svasukhecchaya.
Ye kechit sukhita loke sarve te anyasukhecchaya

(Anyone who focuses on his or her own happiness will always be unhappy. Those who strive to make others happy end up being happy themselves.)

Friendship is all about sharing joys and sorrows. In the previous chapter, we saw how people tend to use others as a means of finding their own happiness, either by pressuring them or by bullying them. In this chapter, we will explore the opposite. How can we become a source of happiness for our friends? How can we bring joy into the lives of our friends? How should we celebrate the joys of our friends? How can we help our friends deal with their sorrows? How can we add value to the lives of our friends?

'Don't walk behind me, I may not lead. Don't walk in front of me; I may not follow. Just walk beside me and be my friend,' wrote French philosopher and author Albert Camus. As he puts it, friendship is about walking together on the long road of life with all its ups and downs. Deep friendships are forged by pulling the mind away from personal needs, interests and concerns and focusing on the needs, interests, and concerns of the one we want to connect with. The connections deepen even further when one learns the art of empathetically listening without judging.

In the Ramayana, we find that Rama practised this principle to perfection, which is why he managed to build so many deep friendships across the country and even across species! What was Rama's secret, which allowed him to influence so many people and win so many friends? Why did they love Rama so much? I would say it was because he participated in their joys and sorrows like they were his own. When there was cause to celebrate, Rama would join in and celebrate with the people of Ayodhya. Being happier than all his citizens! When there was sorrow or failure, Rama would again be present and cry along with his people. Rama did not try to solve his friends' problem but empathized with them. He knew that not all problems could be solved, some just had to be weathered.

Here is a different perspective. Have you thought about what would be a good number of friends to have? One? Five? Fifteen? On social media, people usually have hundreds of friends. Should we set a maximum or a minimum number of friends for ourselves? Saurav had this same question in his mind when he went to his teacher, who was known to be kind and wise. She always had unique ways of explaining things to him.

'Ma'am, how many friends does one really need: one or many?' he asked her.

She mulled over his question and pointed at a mango tree, saying, 'First, can you get me a mango from the highest branch of that tree?'

Saurav looked at the tree towering over him. It seemed like it was touching the sky! Feeling dizzy just angling his neck to look at the tree, he asked, 'How will I ever reach that highest branch?'

'Think about it. Maybe you could ask a friend to help you out,' the teacher suggested.

Saurav asked one of his friends to come to his aid. He then stood on his friend's shoulders to reach a mango on the highest branch. But even their combined height was not enough for him to reach the mango. Disappointed, he looked around for some inspiration.

'Do you have more friends?' the teacher asked.

Saurav called some more of his friends. Together, they tried to form a pyramid with tiers and tiers of boys standing on each other's shoulders. It was a tough task to balance themselves. Soon enough, they all came tumbling down. The high-hanging mango remained elusive and out of reach.

'Saurav, have you understood how many friends you need?'

Saurav was nonplussed: how was fetching the mango related to his question? He thought a bit and said, 'I guess I need many friends so that together we could get the mango?' It was more of a question than a realization.

Laughing at his confusion, the teacher said, 'It's true. You should have as many friends as it takes to find at least one who is smart enough and has the common sense to advise you to bring a ladder!'

It's always good to have at least one wise friend among the crowd of 'fun friends'. Wise friends expand the horizon of our thinking, stretch our minds, prod our conscience and touch our soul. Most friends we hang out with will have nothing notable to tell us in a time of crisis. Think about it: don't most of your conversations revolve around movies, sports, careers, gossip, fun or entertainment? My point is, while all this is fun and important in life, we also need at least one person who says things that go deeper and make us think. The wise friend often knows us better than we know ourselves.

Many times, we face tough questions, like 'why did this happen to me?' When we come across questions this big, just facts don't help—we need the help of wisdom that helps us look beyond what things appear to be. If we have friends who are able to provide that, they become crucial to our mental health and to our emotional quotient.

But wait . . . there's a catch. It is not easy to celebrate the joys and the successes of a friend without jealousy creeping in. It's not easy to be happy when your friend is happy while you are focused on your own happiness. Externally, they may seem to smile and dance when they see your success or joy. But internally, they might be crying over not being as successful themselves or angry at how the other could become successful when they were still struggling. Rare is that friend who is selfless enough to dance joyously without carrying the burden of jealousy in their heart.

We sometimes see that when a person achieves some degree of success or reaches a milestone, it fosters envy and anger. Anger is an adult temper tantrum. Children get angry when they don't get the candy they so desire. Adults, naturally, are not angry about losing out on candies, but it hits hard when they are not the centre of attention and someone else gets all the love and appreciation. The success of a friend might create insecurity and shatter their peace of mind.

Do you know why? Because jealous friends define their worth based on the failure of those around them rather than on their own achievements. The success of those they are close to is unacceptable because it makes them painfully aware of their own failures. In their mind, it highlights their defeat and unworthiness. It kindles heartburn, anxiety and fuels self-crippling fear.

For them, success is possibly a prerequisite for gaining acceptance and a respectable place in society, so the success of another means someone else is going to hog all the attention. The fear of being unsuccessful, and therefore rejected, unloved and inconsequential is so strong that they suffer all their lives long. Jealousy, wherever it may lurk, is always indicative of the same thought pattern. It's essentially characterized by two things: first, the compulsive need for approval and second, an intense feeling of inferiority. A jealous person is jealous because of a lack of self-trust.

You can be jealous of the whole world but not of those you love, not of your friend who trusts you much with their emotions. When it comes to friendship, we need to learn to drop these negative emotions. Let me tell you a sweet story about this.

A crow swooped down just in time to pick up a piece of meat that had fallen off a butcher's shelf. In the blink of an eye, it was gone. No one even noticed the piece had gone missing. Proud of his achievement in tricking the burly butcher, the crow flew to perch on a treetop, where he could relish the magnificent meal in peace. Just as he was about to devour his lunch, he heard an intense, high-pitched squeal that sent a tremor through his every feather. He knew what that meant. He raised his head just in time to see the claws of an eagle rushing towards his face. Reflex action took over and the next moment, the crow was airborne with its prize safely in its claws.

The squeals now multiplied and were coming from several directions. The crow flew for dear life. A horde of eagles was chasing the crow from all sides. A hot pursuit followed. The crow was tiring and the eagles were closing in. Just then, the crow heard a commanding voice instructing him, 'Drop the meat!'

He turned his neck in the direction of the voice and saw his best friend flapping his wings, trying to keep up. The crow was upset at his friend. Instead of helping him deal with the chasing eagles, he was telling him to drop his hard-earned food. Understanding what the crow was thinking, the friend shouted out, 'The eagles are not chasing you. They don't care for you. They are chasing the meat you are holding on to. If you want to remain alive, drop the meat. You can always find something else to eat if you live.'

Realization dawned on the crow. He reluctantly let go of the piece of meat he was holding on to so dearly. As soon as he let go, the eagles swooped downwards, rushing towards the falling meat. Finally landing beside his friend on a tree branch, the crow breathed a sigh of relief. Thanking his friend for his wisdom, the crow decided to remember this timely advice for life.

When negativity seems to be closing in on you and you seem to be struggling for very survival, remember the story of this crow. The solution lies within you. There is something we are holding on to that attracts negativity into our life. And if we just let go of that harmful mindset, what happens? The negativity fades away automatically. Jealousy is just one example of a harmful and self-destructive attitude. The crow was carrying just one piece of meat, but we are carrying many wrong notions that we need to let go of in order to gain meaningful and deep friendships.

People feel most alone when they are very happy or very sad. Someone who stands beside them in such times becomes very dear. But why do peoplen feel lonely when very happy or very sad? Simply because when a person is very happy about an achievement or worldly success, people around him become envious. On the other hand, when a person is low due to some sort of failure or loss, people prefer to stay away from their negative vibes. Often, even close family members do not know how to deal with a person who is very happy or very sad. During such extreme emotions, the human heart is most open to receiving kindness, love, affection, appreciation and genuine comfort. Whoever manages to connect during this time wins a heartfelt friendship.

Renowned author Oscar Wilde had rightly pointed out, 'Anybody can sympathize with the suffering of a friend, but it requires a very fine nature to sympathize with a friend's success.' When someone feels that others want them to succeed, there are greater chances that they might actually succeed. Whereas when someone feels that others want them to fail, it's more likely that they might really fail. Do you know why people do not like to participate in celebrating the success of others? It is the same reason that prevents them from succeeding: a comparative mentality that leads to insecurity and jealousy. When you compare yourself to others who are successful, you always find yourself lacking. In that mindset of insecurity, you bury all your chances of success.

So the question arises, how does one claw out of this self-defeating loop? It's simple. Rather than being jealous of a friend's success and achievements, you should celebrate together. When you really feel happy when your friend is happy, you can call yourself a true friend.

The solution is to begin celebrating others' success. When you begin celebrating others' success, especially of those close to you, you begin to defeat jealousy. Competition is exhausting, and celebration is exhilarating.

When the green-eyed monster raised its head, here's what happened with Vibha and Amrita. They were friends in college. Vibha was a natural leader, academically accomplished and an excellent public speaker. Amrita was artistic and creative, a painter. Though both had different talents, Amrita would feel pangs of envy occasionally, especially when Vibha received recognition for her participation in the inter-collegiate debate. Her confidence and her ability to present her arguments mesmerized the judges. She was always in the limelight for something or the other. And she was the centre of attraction again, standing for the post of captain in the college elections.

It was difficult for Amrita to share Vibha's happiness when she was feeling a cocktail of negative emotions. Was it envy or sadness or anger? Or all three? On analysing her negativity, she came to some conclusions which then helped her conduct herself with dignity. Her first conclusion was that her primary emotion was that of jealousy because she too wanted to be appreciated for her art and she too wanted to be in the spotlight. She was human, after all, and which human being would not want all of that? When this became clear to her, she decided she would accept this feeling rather than sweep it under the carpet. Her next conclusion was that she would not let it affect her relationship with Vibha because Vibha thought of her as her best friend and they had been friends since childhood. What would she have done if she were in Vibha's place? In Vibha's place, she would have expected some help from her friend in campaigning for the elections. Amrita decided to do exactly that. Being an artist, she could easily make posters and banners for Vibha. They were allowed to put them up in the college campus a week before elections. She got down to work to make some huge banners in gold and silver, which would stand out. It took her many days and nights, but it was worth the effort because when she showed them to Vibha, Vibha was so touched by her gesture that she hugged her friend. She clasped her hands and whispered a 'thank you' in her ear. They discussed their campaign strategies together and Amrita stood by her side all throughout, helping her with all the artwork.

Finally, the day dawned when they would find out who the new captain was. Lo and behold, it was none other than Vibha. The new college captain. This time, Amrita did not burn with jealousy but jumped with joy. She could share Vibha's joy because she had been with her in her journey, sharing her burdens and anxieties. They had grown closer than ever before. It was an occasion to celebrate. Her best friend was captain. She went home and baked a huge black forest cake. The next day, when she walked in with the cake to celebrate Vibha's victory, everyone spoke about Amrita's role in Vibha's success. The teachers acknowledged in class how selflessly Amrita had worked for her friend. She was a symbol of friendship. She basked in the limelight, happy to have made herself and her friend proud of their friendship.

The great thinker Chanakya says, 'The test of a servant happens while he performs his duty, the test of a relative is in difficulty, the test of a friend is in adversity and the test of a spouse is in misfortune.' It's very easy to be a fair-weather friend. In fact, when life is fun, there will always be lots of people around you. But when you go through adversity, only a real friend will stand by you. And it isn't easy to be a support to a friend and help him sail through tough times, simply because the negativity of those tough times can break the toughest of people.

If it is you yourself going through a lean phase, it's natural to recognize your own suffering. But when it is a friend who is suffering, it is difficult to think beyond yourself and empathize with your friend's woes. To put yourself in the shoes of another and feel what they feel requires an expansive mindset. Empathy doesn't come easily to adults. But it is much easier for children to empathize with others' pain and suffering. Have you observed small children when they are in an environment of sorrow or where people are crying? They begin to cry without even comprehending what is going on. They just sense the mood and express their emotional reaction to it without any inhibition.

If we want to learn what friendship really means, we can learn from little Vincent. This is a true story of a five-year-old from USA, who learnt that his best friend, Zac, had leukaemia, a form of cancer. He saw how simply playing for many hours with his friend was not enough to cheer him up. He wanted to share the pain of the harrowing process of chemotherapy, which had taken away Zac's hair. So five-year-old Vincent went home and forced his parents to have his head shaved. The parents, of course, refused at first, thinking it was a childish and foolish demand. But when Vincent remained adamant, they sat down and had a heart-to-heart talk with him. Little Vincent said, 'Cancer has made Zac bald and if I also become bald, he will feel he's not the only one.'

His parents were simply blown away by Vincent's sensitivity, his deep sense of empathy and his commitment to friendship. That was not all Vincent did. He got his mother to make scarves and sold them in school to raise money for Zac's expensive chemotherapy. Vincent exemplifies the mind of a true friend, who does everything in his power to share a friend's sorrow. Even cancer became something to smile about when Zac saw his friend's bald head matching his own.

When it comes to empathy, I think kids have got it just right. Because they don't think too much about what the right thing to do is. They just act straight from their hearts. Like little Vedika, who was all of four years old. Her neighbour Simi, also four years of age, was her best friend. They played together, went to school together, laughed and cried together. Outsiders even thought of them as twin sisters. So one day, when her friend Simi just disappeared, Vedika's young mind could not understand what had happened. She only saw Simi's mother crying all the time. Thinking something had happened to Simi, she went and sat in Simi's mother's lap to console her. Overwhelmed by the mother's grief, Vedika started crying. The child's presence and compassion assuaged Simi's mother's sorrow somewhat; she had lost her little Simi in a car accident. Vedika reminded her of her daughter and Simi's mother embraced this child, knowing that Simi still lived in her innocent heart.

Maybe children empathize so spontaneously because they don't use their intelligence to analyse it. Intelligence sometimes acts as the biggest barrier in human relationships.

Intelligence helps you think rationally, but when it comes to relationships, it's important to think emotionally as well as rationally. Those who think emotionally can empathize with others' situations better.

Usually, those who are very talented and knowledgeable have been observed to lack empathy. In Sanskrit, *veda* means knowledge, so one who knows a lot is called a *vedi*. For example, a '*chaturvedi*' is one who knows all the Vedas properly, which essentially means that they are very knowledgeable. The word *vedana* means suffering. Understanding the vedana of others means understanding the suffering of others or being able to empathize with others' pain. It is often seen that those who have veda do not understand the vedana of others. Intelligence is required to understand veda, but emotional intelligence is required to understand vedana.

Our education systems help us develop our intelligence, but unfortunately provide no scope for emotional development. If we want deep friendships, we must develop our emotional intelligence so that we can feel the pain of others. It is not rocket science. Children know intuitively how to empathize with others. We just need to invoke the child in ourselves in order to feel empathy towards our friends.

Acharya Chanakya says something even more significant about friendship: 'He is a true friend who does not forsake us in time of need, misfortune, famine, or war, in a king's court, or at the crematorium.' This simply means that a friend does not give up on his friend no matter what. In every stage of life, a true friend stands by you. This is known to be true even in the animal kingdom.

There are many stories of animals that have honoured their friendships no matter what. Have you heard of this story of the friendship between two lizards in Japan? Let me tell you. Once, a lizard was nailed to a wall by mistake. Naturally, it couldn't move. But what is amazing is that it remained nailed to the wall for the next ten years and still survived. All because it had a little friend who didn't leave its side. You won't believe their friendship! Its friend brought it food every single day for ten long years. When two lizards can do so much for one another, how much more could humans do for each other? We may not always be able to do a lot, but at least we can learn from these lizards and empathize with our friend's difficulties.

If this story didn't inspire you sufficiently to cultivate empathy—especially because it was about lizards—let me tell you the story of Chetak. Chetak's story represents the height of empathy and the depth of friendship. Oh, by the way, Chetak is a horse. Yes, a horse! You may recall his name from history. Chetak belonged to the famous king Maharana Pratap of Chittor. They were inseparable and the best of friends. They understood each other without a single word being exchanged between them. During one of the most important battles in Rana Pratap's life, Chetak was severely injured, losing strength in one of his legs. Despite that, Chetak continued carrying Rana on his back, balancing on three legs. At a point in the war, Rana Pratap was completely overpowered and was losing. Eventually, he fell unconscious on Chetak's back. Comprehending the dangerous situation his friend was in, Chetak began to run away from the battlefield, carrying the unconscious Rana Pratap. Ignoring his own pain, Chetak managed to run far away from the enemies towards a hill. On his three legs, this loyal friend ran up a hill, and when he saw a large stream of water, he jumped across it with all his might, carrying his friend on his back. Chetak died upon landing on the other side, but in the process, he saved the life of his lifelong friend.

Have you ever experienced moments when a friend has stood by you when you were distraught? Standing by a friend during all phases of life is the essence of friendship. Just your presence can be a gratifying experience for a friend. But don't expect this to happen overnight. Every relationship needs to be cultivated and cultivation needs patience. Everything that is invaluable takes time to develop. Look at the most precious pearls on the ocean bed. Fresh water pearls take between one and six years to form and saltwater pearls take between five and twenty years. I am sure you have seen or worn diamond jewellery. But have you ever wondered how long it takes to form diamonds? The answer is shocking. It takes anywhere from 1 to 3.3 billion years to form diamonds. Imagine! When you plant an almond tree, it takes about twelve years to produce good almonds. Sandalwood trees take thirty years to grow before it is ready to be harvested for its fragrant wood. Anything that is of any significance takes time. When it comes to something as valuable as friendship, it similarly takes a lot of patience and nurture.

Patience is most required when we need to help a friend deal with their sorrows and troubles. I want to share a very interesting verse from the Ramayana that talks about what sorrows do to a human being.

Shoko nashyate dhairya shoko nashyate shrutam
Shoko nashyate sarvam naasti shokasamo ripuh

(Sorrow kills one's patience. Sorrow destroys one's ability to discriminate between right and wrong, good and bad. Sorrow whisks away all good qualities that one may have. Thus, sorrow is one's biggest enemy. One should never submit to the clutches of sorrow.)

The above verse was said by Kaushalya to Rama, her son, who was about to leave for the forest, exiled from the kingdom. She was extremely sad about the decision that her husband had taken. In that distressed state of mind, she had spoken harsh words to her husband. With reference to her harsh words, she tells Rama about the nature of sorrow and to what extent sorrow can affect the human heart.

But keeping one's head in sorrow is easier said than done. It is very difficult to remain mentally stable once you have fallen into the whirlpool of sorrow. Sadness can shatter your peace and equanimity. The inability to handle sadness and failure eventually pushes people into depression. Most youngsters who end up chronically depressed after sorrow seek psychiatric or psychological help when it is beyond their capacity to handle these emotions. Taking anti-depressants is common among the youth these days. But what can your few minutes with a counsellor do? Professional counsellors are not always with you and not always available when you need them. Many times, they might even lack the sensitivity to handle tender and fragile emotions.

This is the unfortunate situation today. Smiling faces, crying hearts. If you ask anyone 'how are you?' everyone will immediately say, 'I am fine.' But the fact is that behind those smiling faces is an ocean of misery. What they really need is a tender human heart ready to listen to their worries and anxieties with empathy and without judgement. Sometimes, what professional counselling cannot achieve, a friend who is genuinely interested in you can. Unfortunately, most youngsters are not ready to open their hearts to their friends, siblings or parents because they have not invested time or energy in building bonds with real people. They have not given importance to being good friends. Genuine friends are, in fact, the best counsellors. Sometimes, talking to a true friend can do what no professional can. The only thing that is needed of us is the courage to tell them, 'I need help.' Unfortunately, doing that is not easy. It requires guts. It requires you to overcome your insecurities and fears of being judged as weak. It requires you to trust them with your secrets and weaknesses.

Here is a story to illustrate how hard it can be to admit to our shortcomings. A new circus had arrived in a small village. The way it was advertised managed to catch everybody's attention: 'Come and see the circus for just 25 paise!' The entire village was thrilled. Nothing was available for 25 paise, and yet here was a circus advertising itself for that tiny sum. The first show attracted a massive crowd and there was a huge line outside the ticket counter. Almost the entire village assembled to witness the cheapest circus ever. With great excitement, the first person stepped into the circus tent holding his ticket in his hand, expecting an exciting array of performances for his entertainment. To his surprise, the tent was empty. No performers! He turned around and saw that the entrance had been shut. Only one person was allowed to enter at a time. While he was wondering what was happening, a burly wrestler entered the tent from the other end and walked towards him. This was getting frustrating. Unable to tolerate the suspense anymore, he walked up to the wrestler and demanded an explanation. He had paid to see a good show and he wanted to see it. The wrestler smiled and in the next moment, gave him a tight slap across the cheek. Grinning sarcastically, he said, 'What did you expect for 25 paise?'

The first spectator walked out after being slapped by the wrestler. Everyone waiting in line looked confused but wanted to know about his experience. Not wanting to accept that he had been beaten up and not wanting to admit that he was a fool to believe in the '25 paisa for the circus' advertisement, he praised the show profusely. The crowd's expectations rose exponentially and so did its enthusiasm. Soon, everyone from the village attended the circus (and got beaten up). Yet, no one was ready to admit that they had made a mistake and had been foolish to believe the advertisement. Each person would go in, get slapped, come out of the tent and sing the show's praises to the next person.

Such is the nature of human beings. We are constantly in denial of our weaknesses, failures, defeats and shortcomings. Sure, one need not accept it in front of the world, but there should be at least one friend with whom one can share everything. A true friend will never take advantage of your weaknesses, but will take care of you.

A lonely person only has his own mind for company. And the mind is not necessarily always a good friend. In fact, sometimes, we might even make the most foolish decisions in life in emotionally charged moments.

Your mind and your intelligence are two separate entities, not one! In routine life, our intelligence is in charge of the decision-making process, but in emotionally demanding situations, like those that arise on occasions of great joy or in tough times of sorrow, the mind, being the emotional centre, takes over. When the mind takes over, all decisions that are taken are not based on careful consideration but on your feelings. And these decisions are often emotional because facts are neglected when feelings are placed at the forefront of the decision-making process. That's when one needs to borrow intelligence. When our personal intelligence is not of much use, having been dominated by the emotional mind, it's a good idea to use the intelligence of a trusted friend.

In this context, do you know what the Bhagavadgita is? It is simply a discussion between an emotionally disturbed friend and a supportive, intelligent friend. Arjuna was caught in an emotional dilemma that he wasn't able to resolve, no matter how much he contemplated it. It was arguably the most critical moment in his life as a warrior and his defining moment as a leader. His decision would affect the lives of countless people, both on the battlefield and off it. It was not just the present that was at stake, but the future of governance itself for decades to come.

However, what made Arjuna extraordinary was that he knew and recognized that he was in a highly charged frame of mind and that it wasn't the best state in which to make critical decisions. It is not enough to accept that your mind is confused, you must also have the humility to admit it to another person and seek help. In spite of his position as a renowned warrior and leader, he had the courage and humility to tell his friend that he was confused and needed help. Krishna immediately empathized with his friend's situation and discoursed on the entire scenario from various different angles. Those various perspectives are compiled in what we know today as the Bhagavadgita. Krishna not only helped Arjuna deal with the negativity in his mind but also added tremendous value to his life through his empathetic and non-judgemental delivery of unparalleled wisdom.

When we are too close to a problem, our vision tends to blur. Only when we see the problem from a distance can we see it with clarity. When we are unable to achieve the distance to look at the problem objectively, it is best to invite a friend to help us do so. Here is another story that will help you understand this concept.

Kaivalya was in college when he first started gambling. It gave him a high when he won a couple of thousand rupees easily. Beginner's luck, some said, but he believed he would not run out of it. Doesn't everyone fall into that trap? And when he started losing, he broke down. The graph dove as dramatically as it had soared. Before he knew it, he owed the casino two lakh rupees. Where would a student get so much money from? Credit to him for not thinking of stealing or committing any crimes. Instead, he had the good sense to confide in his friend, Abhay, a practical guy who would surely have some good ideas.

Abhay's first reaction was, 'Have you told your father?'

'Oh no,' came the reply. 'If I tell him, I'm dead.'

'Yes, you will get maybe a lecture on the problems of gambling, but in the long run, he is the safest person to confide in and take money from,' Abhay explained.

Kaivalya was reluctant to take that advice. How would he face his father? How would his father trust him again? But Abhay said, 'Kaivalya, you are considering only one aspect. You're wondering, if you borrow money from someone, how will you pay them back? And if you don't, that person will threaten you, the loan will keep accumulating, the interest will keep adding up and you will have to pay much more by the time you get the money together. Eventually, you will have to go to your father, and after having faced even more difficulties. Why not go now? Apologize to him and assure him you will not venture into gambling again. I'm sure he will forgive you. It's not just a question of money; it's also a matter of admitting you made a mistake and coming clean.' Abhay added, 'I will come with you to vouch for you.'

The more Kaivalya thought about it, the more sense it made to him. Mustering courage, he and Abhay confessed to his father. As expected, his father was upset. But he appreciated that Kaivalya was brave enough to admit his mistake. He also praised Kaivalya for having friends like Abhay who provided the right perspective so that Kaivalya could take the right steps to rectify his error. Had it not been for Abhay's take on the problem, Kaivalya would have suffered tremendously.

Everyone has dreams, but when we come across hurdles and failures, our gaze drifts away from our dream. But just like a good friend provides sensible advice when we are overcome with emotion, a good friend also doesn't allow our focus to drift away from our dreams. Instead, a friend like that helps us deal with the problem and gently brings our attention back to our dream. When we encourage the dreams of others, we encourage friendship to grow. A friend is a friend when they add value to a friend's life. There is no shortage of detractors. What everyone really needs is someone who can bolster our optimism. Giving up is the easiest thing to do. Getting up after a fall is the toughest. It becomes easy when lovingly encouraged, and friendship is all about encouragement.

How do you encourage a friend? Often, it is simply by being present during the most important times of a friend's life. The highest form of encouragement is vocalizing your appreciation.

The Ramayana is a classic story of friendship. Rama travelled across the country befriending people. He probably made the most striking and unlikely friends. He simply followed one principle that made him a universally popular friend. He valued people and appreciated them wholeheartedly. Those that were rejected by everyone, including their own family members, Rama accepted unconditionally.

Sugriva was from the Vanara clan and in the middle of a massive tiff with his brother Vali, or Bali, as he is commonly known, when Rama came into his life. Vali had prohibited Sugriva from entering the kingdom, taken away his right to any inheritance, ordered that he be killed and kidnapped his wife, all over a small mistake. What a severe punishment over an understandable error! When his kith and kin had rejected him, Sugriva saw no hope of being accepted anywhere any longer. He lived on a lonely mountaintop, hanging feebly on to dear life. He had lost all hope, all direction and all purpose. The first thing Rama did as soon as he met Sugriva was to establish trust in their friendship. Rama embraced Sugriva so lovingly that the Vanara's heart melted. His family had rejected him, but here was a stranger who was accepting him unconditionally as a friend. Rama focused on giving Sugriva hope. Once hope came back into Sugriva's life, Rama helped him find a purpose. Once he had both hope and a sense of purpose, slowly, his confidence returned as well. But Rama didn't leave his side just yet. He stayed with him and helped Sugriva regain everything he had lost.

The average person is most helpless in two phases of life. One is when they are born. At that time, their parents help them survive. The other phase of helplessness comes later in life, when their confidence in their own selves hits rock bottom. This helplessness could be due to anything: a fallout, heartbreak, old age, etc. At this time, you need a friend who can help you overcome your helplessness. Parents help you due to a blood relationship, because it's their duty. But why does a friend need to help you? There is no obligation whatsoever. There is no blood connection either. There is a heart-to-heart connection, which can prove to be many times stronger than blood relationships in some cases.

Yet another classic story of friendship in the Ramayana is that of Rama with Vibhishana, the younger brother of the king of Lanka, Ravana. Though Vibhishana was extremely intelligent and had great foresight, Ravana never valued his brother. In Lanka, it always had to be Ravana's way. Everyone had to value his opinions, likes and dislikes. When Vibhishana once expressed his opinion and opposed Ravana's foolhardy decision, he was humiliated and kicked out. In Lanka, there was a zero-tolerance policy for disagreements with the king. At this point, Vibhishana had two options: to stay in Lanka after apologizing to his brother, or living a life of dignity but uncertainty. He chose the second option as that would not tarnish his self-image. He felt that up to that point, he had always done what his brother wanted him to do, but from then on, he wanted to do what he felt was right.

That was when he decided to do the unheard of. He walked straight into the enemy camp. Rama was the sworn enemy of Lanka and therefore, of anyone coming from there. Interestingly, when Rama heard that Vibhishana had decided to leave his brother's camp because he felt that his brother was wrong, Rama did not hesitate to embrace him. The entire army was stunned, most of all Vibhishana himself. How could an enemy accept him so gracefully when his own sibling had rejected him and demeaned him? For Rama, it wasn't simply military strategy. He genuinely connected with anyone he felt could be his friend. In fact, he called Vibhishana his own brother. Not only did Rama accept him, he added great value to his life. In the next seven days that they were together, waging the war against Lanka, Vibhishana learnt the most valuable lessons of his life just by observing Rama's dealings with his soldiers, brother and friends. Vibhishana felt that he had learnt more from Rama in those seven days than he had learnt in his entire life in Lanka.

To make a friend for life, one first needs to be aware of the person's current mindset. People tend to be intimately connected to certain life events and what they do or say is linked to these experiences. The easiest way to touch their hearts is to reach that place in their heart. Rama could touch Sugriva and Vibhishana's hearts so deeply because he had already divined their current emotional state. They were both fighting rejection by their respective families. They were both low on self-esteem. They were both looking for some value in themselves after living in the shadow of their brothers all their lives. They both needed a little love, a sense of belonging. Once Rama understood where their hearts were, he had only to walk to that point and they gave themselves to him in friendship. Therefore, the lesson from Rama's conduct is this: if you want to add value to your friendships, you need to value your friends first.

Like Mark Twain has said, 'Keep away from people who try to belittle your ambitions. Small people always do that, but the really great make you feel that you, too, can become great.' Everyone needs someone who believes in them. The path to greatness begins with encouragement. It's not just enough to encourage with words, however. Behind those encouraging words, there has to be a pair of caring arms that are ready to catch you when you fall and embrace you in celebration. Can you name a single person who has achieved any kind of success without encouragement and care? The interesting thing is, when you help one person, his gratitude results in him helping many more people achieve success, thereby setting off a positive chain reaction.

A good friend doesn't just add value to your life but also helps you find yourself when you feel lost in the journey of life. An example of this is the following story.

There were rumours doing the rounds in college that Ajay's friend Ravi did drugs. When the rumours reached Ajay's ears, he was flabbergasted. Ravi had been Ajay's best friend since the beginning of college and to the best of his knowledge, he had never taken drugs. These rumours spread like wildfire, though, and every student in college would peep into their class to see who Ravi was. They would stare at him in the corridors. Juniors gawked at him as if he were an alien. Ajay tried to dismiss these rumours, but they refused to die out. Every day, they were destroying Ravi's self-confidence bit by bit. The humiliation, the isolation, the scathing comments were too much to handle. It was then that Ajay decided to step in and help his friend. At that point, Ravi seemed too shaken to think straight and was heading towards a nervous breakdown. Ajay took Ravi to the principal and explained the situation to him. From Ravi's haggard appearance, the principal realized it was a serious matter. Ajay gave him all the details and the principal took immediate action. The trouble makers were directly handled by the principal and warned not to malign him. Thanks to Ajay's timely intervention,

Ravi was able to overcome depression. Friends like Ajay who make level-headed decisions in times when you are unable to do so can add immense value to the quality of your life.

Similarly, when Maria's ex-boyfriend started making threatening calls to her, she became severely anxious. Living all alone in a metro city, she felt vulnerable. Her only pillar of support was her best friend, who was in another city. But the minute Maria told her about the threatening phone calls, her friend dropped everything to be with her. She got her cell number changed, moved her to a different house and made her file a police complaint against the boyfriend. Maria would never have been able to do all this by herself. Only when Maria felt safe and secure did her friend return.

Have you been a friend like Ajay? Join the exclusive club of givers today! There are already enough takers in the world.

Summary:

- It's not the quantity of friendship that matters but the quality of it.
- Jealousy and insecurity mar the beauty of true friendship.
- Those who understand the suffering of others are able to empathize with others' pain.
- Learn to be a true friend by adding value to your friendship. Make friends with people who do the same for you.

Activity

You have come across the following sentences in Chapter 6. Fill in the missing words from the pool of given words to reinforce the thoughts.

1. Anyone who focuses on their own happiness will always be _____. Those who strive to make others happy end up being _____ themselves.

2. Anybody can sympathize with the suffering of a friend, but it requires someone evolved to truly celeberate a friend's _____.

3. When you really feel happy in your friend's happiness, you can call yourself a _____ friend.

4. Competition is exhausting while _____ is exhilarating.

5. The test of a worker happens while he performs his _____, the test of a relative is in times of _____, the test of a friend is during _____ and the test of a _____ is in misfortune.

6. When we encourage the dreams of others, we encourage our friendship to _____.

7. Several surveys suggest that being _____ and feeling valued are more important to people than being paid money.

8. To win a lifelong friend, one first needs to find out what is the person's current _____.

> duty unhappy success failure appreciated love celebration happy true difficulty grow adversity spouse mind-set tolerant blaming, bandhu

Answers

1. Unhappy, happy
2. Success
3. True
4. Celebration
5. Duty, difficulty, adversity, spouse
6. Grow
7. Appreciated
8. Mindset

7

Friendships beyond Friends

Friendship need not only be with friends. As you may have noticed, friendship is more than just a relationship—it is an attitude and a way of life. Keeping this in mind, the concept of friendship can be extended beyond just your friends. In this chapter, we will explore four ways in which the basic values of friendship can be used in relationships other than those between peers.

1. Friendship with parents
2. Friendship with animals
3. Being your own best friend
4. Online friendships

Remember that the quality of your interactions with the world outside you determines your success and the quality of your interactions with the world inside you determines your happiness. So far in this book, we have discussed peer interactions and friendships. Now we will discuss interactions with parents, with other friends and, most importantly, with yourself.

Parents as Friends

Teenage is the most important period in human development. It is characterized by a desperate struggle to comprehend who you are and what the purpose of your life is. While you are still trying to understand yourself, everyone else around you, especially your parents, constantly tell you who you are or who you should be. Half your energy and time, then, is spent disagreeing with them. The other half is spent recognizing and accepting yourself for who you discover you actually are. In the middle of this process of self-discovery, temptations keep hurling you into turbulent waters.

Let me share with you some thoughts on how you can improve your relationship with your parents. Just like parents spend a lot of time trying to learn how to raise their kids well, I feel that there is a lot for a child to learn too.

Frankly speaking, you may never find better friends than your parents. There, I said it! Before you shake your head—which is a justified reaction—let me assure you that I say this based on my personal experience. You will certainly find many good friends. You might even find best friends. But I can guarantee you, no one can outdo your parents in being your friends and supreme well-wishers.

Do you know what the most difficult part of parenting is? You! Parenting is not easy. You do not realize how difficult you are till you find somebody just like you. If you had to take care of someone as headstrong and finicky as yourself, do you think you would be willing to? For example, every parent feels that the biggest reason for their son's or daughter's indifference towards them is their mobile phone. On the other hand, most young people feel that their phones have given them independence and access to a whole new world. It is the inability of either side to put themselves in the shoes of the other and view the same thing through different lenses that has caused such a generation gap. What you are about to read now will change the way you look at your parents forever. Please bear with me and read this section with an open mind and the desire to reconnect with your earliest, truest friends.

Did you know that nearly all emotional problems that adults go through later in life are somehow or the other connected with their relationship with their parents? Psychological research acknowledges the existence of an invisible bond that binds us to our families long after our parents stop being our caretakers. This connection to our parents is one of the most important energy powerhouses of our life—each time we reconnect to this source, we are charged with great amounts of energy, which then impacts all aspects of our lives positively. The opposite is equally powerful: each time we neglect this source, we are drained of that energy and instead are filled with negativity that pushes us into depressive and abnegating thought processes.

The bond that a living being shares with its source, its parents, is a bond that nourishes for life. The first wave of loving emotions that we experienced in life was towards our mother and the second was towards our father. Those emotions were the seed from which all other emotions we have experienced have emerged. No matter how sour or bad or indifferent our relationship with our parents turns out to be as we grow up, the original bond can never be severed. In fact, there are so many forms of therapy today that are based on this. When people go through problems or suffer from prolonged ailments, mental disorders, relationship issues, anxiety, loneliness, etc., they are recommended to work on their relationship with their parents and when they do that, many times, their problems are automatically resolved. The dynamics in human dealings are essentially a subtle form of energy exchange.

When two people have an argument or a misunderstanding or don't get along with each other, the energy exchange is rocky, unstable. The energy between them constantly gets stuck around blocks and does not move freely. The closer these two people, the more disturbed the energy patterns and their effect on these people's lives. In many cases, these energy disturbances last for days and in some cases, for years. These disturbed energy patterns affect the quality of our life and future relationships. The energy disturbances between parents and their children are the most powerful influence in every aspect of the children's lives.

Keeping this in mind, let us see how you can perceive your relationship with your parents as a teenager or an adolescent, when the relationship begins to strain and fray, usually for the first time. When a child is born, it looks for a hero who can protect it. It finds a hero in its parents. It naively assumes that they are infallible heroes who could never be wrong or do wrong. That heroic image of the parents remains in the child's mind for several years till it begins to observe the obvious and not-so-obvious failings of these heroes. Based on these observations, the child, now an adult, begins to form judgements about their parents, often not allowing the opposing side to clarify. Life would be easy if these heroes always remained heroes in the eyes of their children. Unfortunately, parents are not heroes but human beings with limitations. The only speciality of these humans is that, despite their shortcomings, they, more often than not, strive to give their children the best life they possibly can, making great sacrifices that might never be spoken about, simply because they consider it their duty to be selfless. Only when we learn to accept people with their limitations do we actually accept them completely. If parents were perfect, they would never make mistakes and would know exactly what, how and when to say to their children in a way that conflict could be avoided and they could continue to appear heroic. But because they are imperfect, they may sometimes end up saying the wrong things in the wrong way and at the wrong time, causing intense bouts of irritation in a young mind. If only they were perfect!

Some parents' struggles are even more complicated. They appear to be failures in one or every aspect of their own lives, including career, relationships, health, family, sometimes even in their own eyes. Some may, for this reason, become emotionally and/or physically abusive. Some are addicts and unable to give up their bad habits. When you grow up in environments like these, you miss out on the gentle love, affection and protection that a home is supposed to offer you and though you may see your parents every day, almost always, you end up feeling lonely. Surely, there is no question of befriending such parents? When there is uncertainty in a person's behaviour, it is best to stay away till you feel equipped to help them with their issues instead of being affected by them and causing yourself harm. There is never a question of putting up with abuse of any sort. Relationships can develop only when there is mutual respect between two individuals.

The easiest way is to break away from those who behave badly with us. But that is not always possible, and so, a better way might be to try to understand why they behave the way they do. It is possible that the reason they behave badly with you is because they were ill-treated by their own parents when they were young. It is possible that what they saw is what they learnt and what they learnt is the only way they know to live and behave. If they are addicted to drinking, there's a good chance that they saw alcoholism closely, at home, and find solace in it for that reason. If they are violent, there is a strong possibility that they were dealt with violently in their childhood.

Most people who become parents are actually unprepared for the enormous responsibility that parenthood brings with it. Some of them have yet to mature and grow out of their childish mindsets when they suddenly find themselves saddled with the responsibility of raising and moulding a child. By the time they really get a handle on what it means to be a parent, the child would likely have become a teenager. Now, they are faced with a totally different person, whom they are neither used to nor capable of dealing with, in the body of their grown-up child. So, you see, being a parent is not as easy as you think. Your parents need help too!

Here are some thoughts on how you could help your parents become better parents and better human beings. These are very simple suggestions. They may actually seem too simple, but if you try them out, I am sure you will experience a tremendous difference in the way you perceive your parents and in the quality of the interactions you have with them, no matter what age or stage of life you are at.

1. *Help them become better versions of themselves:* The first thing you need to understand is that parents need your help in becoming better versions of themselves. You may not realize it, but as their children, you have a tremendous influence on your parents. In fact, any parent will confirm that becoming a mother or a father is the single most powerful moment of their lives. You can never comprehend the impact your birth has had on their lives. Imagine, if that is the kind of impact you had on their lives just by being born, how much your word can affect them when articulated thoughtfully. Many parents have given up lifelong self-destructive habits just to get their child's approval. Use the power you have over them to help them become better human beings and better parents. You can achieve what the rest of the world failed to. You can help them when they themselves are helpless

against their vices. You are their second chance at having a nurturing home.

2. *Be compassionate:* As I said before, most parents are totally unprepared and unequipped to handle parenting. The only style of parenting they are comfortable with is the traditional style, in which parents order and their children obey. When their own kids refuse to listen to them or do not care to follow their instructions, their lack of parenting experience and knowledge frustrates them and they don't know how to react. Just to regain control, they begin to scream and dominate. They don't mean to do any of that, but they just run out of ideas. When you don't agree with something they expect you to do, rather than challenging them, try to communicate with them like you would with somebody your own age and with compassion.

3. *Remember that they mean well:* An important point to remember is that whatever parents do for you and ask of you is always for your benefit. There is absolutely nothing they suggest that doesn't come from the concern they feel for you. Even the discipline they impose on you is for your own benefit, even though it may not make sense just then. A study conducted among prison inmates revealed that absolutely every single person interviewed wished that their parents had disciplined them better when they were children. For many, a lack of discipline is what led them astray. Though, at that moment, it may seem cruel and heartless of your parents to discipline you, remember that they are preparing you for a better life, where you

will need to become self-disciplined and they will not be in a position to watch over you. When they expect you to take up small responsibilities and assist them with household chores, they are actually preparing you to handle bigger responsibilities and challenges of your own.

4. *Express your gratitude:* The one thing every parent hopes for and craves to hear from their grown-up son or daughter is a few words of appreciation. When we were little, our parents used to heap words of encouragement and appreciation on us for every little thing we achieved. Even the silliest of mistakes we made—mispronouncing words, the struggles we underwent when we were learning to walk—everything was met with encouragement. Not to mention the millions of sacrifices they made to protect you and care for you. As we grow up and our ability to handle ourselves improves, the desire to be independent also increases. But in return for all our parents' support, it is only reasonable that we spend a few moments with them each day, telling them just how grateful we are for everything they have done for us. We need not always speak. Just being a part of their lives and doing something with them—something as small as washing dishes with your mother or helping your father water the plants—is good enough.

5. *Locate the intention behind a reaction:* When your parents talk to you, try to think about their intention rather than just reacting to their words. Often, we are so caught up in what was said that we forget it may not always be

the same as what was meant. When your mother raises her voice, she is driven by her concern for you. What we say and what we mean to say are two very different things. Your parents may not be able to speak to you the exact same way a friend would. Just because they express their concerns differently, don't interpret that as their desire to control you. Sometimes, their concern may seem exaggerated. But such is the nature of love! Love does tend to become overly protective and sometimes, even irrational. Rather than getting into an argument with them, try to look at their struggle to ensure you are safe. Let us not compete with our parents in arguments; instead, let us appreciate their concerns.

6. *Stop judging, start introspecting:* Rather than always judging your parents for their parenting skills, for once, try to inspect yourself for signs that you are a good son or daughter. Every time we have a heated argument with our parents, we begin to mentally question their ability to be good parents at all. Immediately, your mind begins to hanker for freedom from the parent-child bondage or starts to draw comparisons between your parents and those of your friends or neighbours. While we continue to judge our parents for every mistake they make, do we ever judge ourselves on how we fulfil our responsibilities towards them as their children? When have we ever asked ourselves if we are playing our roles as children properly?

7. *Spend some technology-free time with them:* In 1998, a survey by the *Weekend* magazine in the USA, covering a broad spectrum of teenagers, revealed that the two

biggest influences in their lives were first, parents, and second, religion. If the same survey were to be conducted today, surely, the two biggest influences in a teenager's life would be their mobile phones first and their friends, second. Can we not give our parents, who have given us everything in life, a little more importance than our mobile phones? If that is too much to ask, at least you could start by giving them your undivided attention for a few minutes every day. That's the least we can do to say 'thank you'.

8. *Respect their life experience:* Always remember that your parents are better placed to understand the goings-on of your own life than even you. Even if you have a million friends, the people who will always stand by your side are your parents. Friends come and go like the seasons. But your parents never really leave and never give up on you. They will neither hurt you deliberately, nor break up with you. You may not think of them as cool or smart; they may not be savvy with technology; but they are always there, come rain or shine.

Friendship with Yourself

You may have friends all over the world, but what about being friends with your own self? If you do not befriend yourself, you will always feel lonely and will crave company. After your parents, you are your own best well-wisher. If you can't rely on yourself, why would the world rely on you? If you don't value yourself, why would others value you? When you don't value yourself, you limit your potential. Friendship with oneself begins with finding one's true potential.

A good friend is one who understands a friend very well. If you really want to be your own good friend, you must begin your journey of self-discovery right now. The more you understand yourself, the better friend you will prove to be—not just to yourself but to others as well. A good friend will not allow you to get caught up in a web of negative influences that ruin your potential; friendship with yourself will help you develop a healthy body, mind, intelligence and soul, and act in your best interests.

There is no denying that any form of addiction is an illness. Why would a perfectly healthy person willingly ruin his/her own body? There are statutory warnings on cigarette packs that say, 'Cigarette smoking is injurious to health'. But does that act as a deterrent? Usually, no. A UN World Drug Report found that drug use and associated harm were higher among young people than among the old. A survey done in Delhi in 2018 revealed that nine- and ten-year-olds had already started consuming tobacco and alcohol, while heroin or opium addiction started at the young age of twelve-thirteen years.

Developing an addiction comes with a series of concerns. Addiction is self-abuse, whether it is addiction to drugs, alcohol, cigarettes or gambling. Drug abuse, in particular, takes as great a toll on the body as it does on the mind. Self-abuse can cause serious harm to the body, with the effects lasting even for a lifetime in several cases. In

India, seven people commit suicide per day due to drugs-and addiction-related problems.

The physical impact of substance abuse tends to worsen over time.

Just like there are some habits that destroy the health of the body, there are those that destroy the health of the mind. If you really want to be your own good friend, you must regulate the thoughts that enter your mind through multiple channels. A healthy mind is dependent on the quality of your thoughts. Thoughts, when not monitored, tend towards the negative. Your thoughts are fed into your mind subconsciously through various mediums. The movies you watch and the books you read form the basis of the narrative about life and its various aspects that plays in your mind. When you watch too much violence, you subconsciously become volatile. The mind is like a sponge; it absorbs whatever is dropped onto it.

And do you know of another major addiction? It is addiction to pornography, the favourite pastime of millions of web surfers, most of whom have no idea that they are not only harming themselves but are also contributing to the exploitation of others. Sadly, child porn is one of the fastest growing industries today.

What is seen visually is absorbed by the mind and converted into opinions and thoughts. Thoughts then manifest themselves as words and actions. The vulgarity of the language used by the younger generation is a special indicator of the quality of thoughts in their tender minds. When you constantly watch movies that are riddled with abusive language that becomes part of the vocabulary you use when you talk and think. Even if you don't talk using that vocabulary, out of regard for how others may feel, you will invariably find yourself thinking in or at least about that vocabulary and your opinions and decisions *will* be influenced by it. Bad words that spew out of the mouth destroy your conscience, your ability to distinguish between right and wrong, and lead to heavy mental health challenges like loss of self-respect.

What pornography does is even worse and has a deeper impact. It affects the way you look at the people you are romantically interested in. Once one gets addicted to porn, it becomes difficult to respect your romantic interests and see them as people with a right to choice and dignity, and not objects meant to bring you pleasure.

Can this be stopped? Why not? It's a supply-demand industry and if demand stops, so will the supply. Why demand something that harms your personal life, damages your relationships and, as a result, is detrimental to society? The buck stops here, with you.

A healthy mind thrives on healthy inputs that help it produce a healthy output. Input is received by the mind through the five senses: the eyes, the ears, the nose, the mouth and the skin. The healthier the inputs, the healthier the output, or one's thoughts and desires. There are four types of thoughts that arise in the mind and a balance of these thoughts makes a healthy mind that is friends with itself.

The four types of thoughts are:

1. Necessary thoughts
2. Wasteful thoughts

3. Negative thoughts
4. Positive thoughts

Necessary thoughts are routine thoughts that help you get through your day. Thoughts connected to your work, eating, commuting, schedule, etc., which you use on a regular basis, are known as necessary thoughts. They keep you functioning and are important to get you through your day.

As soon as a wasteful thought appears in a remote corner of our mind, it infects our mind with worry. They come at the wrong time, when we least need them. When wasteful thoughts enter, peace exits. Such thoughts keep repeating themselves in many different ways, just like thoughts of porn, and from many different angles. They are usually about things that we can do nothing about. The only thing these thoughts end up doing is destroying your ability to focus on things that you *can* do something about. These thoughts weaken you, exhaust you and frustrate you.

Wasteful thoughts give birth to more dangerous thoughts: negative thoughts. If wasteful thoughts plant seeds of destruction, negative thoughts ensure that destruction is done. They arise from unsatisfied expectations. These negative thoughts arise from lust, anger, greed, pride and attachment. Negative thoughts are formed by the quality of the input your mind has received. If pornography has been the input, lustful negative thoughts are generated in the mind. If violent movies have been the input, angry or violent thoughts are generated in the mind. Negative thoughts usually encourage criticism and fault-finding.

One ends up finding fault with everyone around them and eventually, criticizing them. Once negative thoughts and negative words enter your life, you begin to actively damage your relationships. Unless you fill up your life with positivity, there is no chance of living a life of quality.

Positive thoughts are those that bring you back to life. They connect you to your original, pure self, which is uninterested in self-destructive, mind-numbing habits. Positive thoughts help us gain access to our inner strength and positive attitudes, and allow us to work towards our best interests. Positive thoughts help us get in touch with the realities of life and pull us out of the illusory world of negativity and selfishness. They help us accept ourselves and others with respect and dignity.

Be a good friend to yourself by monitoring what you put into the mind, thereby controlling the types of thoughts that are produced. When you give a positive input, you get positive results. It's difficult, but not impossible, to generate positive thoughts. Don't lock the potential of your mind by trapping it in a mire of degrading thoughts. A good friend helps you develop a healthy intelligence. Healthy intelligence is developed by sharpening your knowledge and learning continuously. Intelligence is numbed when you stop learning. Most youngsters think it is a good idea to stop learning once they are out of school and university. Everyone spends hundreds of hours in schools and colleges acquiring knowledge, much of which we never use in our lives. Though that knowledge and degree will help you earn your livelihood, you also need knowledge that helps you gain in everyday life. The knowledge I am talking about is not theoretical knowledge, which can be gained from books, but life wisdom. Many talented people who have not invested time and energy in life education find themselves unequipped to handle the challenges that life throws at them. Every day, you have to invest some time in self-upgradation. The 'L' for learner sign on your vehicle may be taken off once you have learnt to drive, but the learner sign on life can never be taken off; you can never learn everything there is to know.

A good friend helps you develop a healthy soul. The development of your soul includes everything from your integrity to your ethics and the development of your faith. Today, as our entire emphasis has shifted to economic growth, value development has taken a back seat. The definition of virtues and ethics has changed drastically and is being twisted to suit people's own agendas. Any talk about faith in anything higher is misconstrued. When we spend some time every day nourishing our souls, we become much better human beings. I am not talking about throwing yourself into institutionalized religion, which encourages hatred towards those who do not believe in it. I am talking about faith that unites; faith in a simple truth that the greatest happiness in this world lies in giving and not taking. The nature of our soul is to serve. The nature of the selfish mind is to take. The moment we decide to spend some time serving selflessly every day, we are making the decision to spend a few moments nourishing our soul. A healthy soul can never exploit another person. A healthy soul can never cross the line of ethics and step into the zone of greed. A healthy soul can never sell its loyalty to God in exchange for some cheap thrills of this world.

Friendship with Animals

If you thought only humans could be your friends, think again. As a famous saying goes, 'Dog is man's best friend!' We are surrounded by animals, especially here in India, and you can see that most people have a very close relationship with animals. Humans are innately drawn towards animals. Could it be because they give unconditional love and bring us great joy?

Research does suggest that desire for a trusted companion runs deep in all animals, humans included. Animals desire companionship as much as we do. And that makes it a mutually advantageous friendship. We have all experienced how complicated human relationships are (that's why you are reading this book!). And that is a good enough reason to have simpler creatures such as animals as our friends.

I know of a cat that runs enthusiastically to meet her human best friend when she sees him; a dog that won't eat till his best friend, the owner, eats with him. Another dog snuck out of his house to meet his human friend in the hospital. A parrot I know of sulks when left alone. I have seen videos of animals rushing to hug their human friends or paying their respects when humans have helped them in any way. There are so many recordings of dogs meeting their owners after years and then going absolutely ecstatic with joy! Such heart-warming videos are shared over and over again on social media.

And in history, we have tales of animal best friends such as Chetak, whom I have mentioned before, and many other furry favourites of great men and women. Animals celebrate with you, share your sorrows, allow you to speak without interrupting you, offer comfort and ask for nothing in return. They know when you're feeling sad, scared, excited or hurt and may even act accordingly. They don't ask questions, they don't pass judgements. Who wouldn't want a friend like that?

Scientists speak of the 'pet effect', the human-animal bond. Pet effect is the positive influence that pets have on their friends. Be it mental health, heart health, immunity— their friendship has benefitted human beings across the entire gamut of health. The presence of animals simply makes our life healthier and happier. This positive impact on our physiology, 'the pet effect', is further proof that animals are our best friends. Let me tell you a heartening story about this unique friendship.

There is a man in a remote village in India who takes care of many cows. He narrates his observations of humans interacting with cows. There was once a lunatic who was roaming the streets of his village. He decided to bring him to his cowshed. As soon as the lunatic entered the cowshed and began touching the cows, he became visibly calmer. He began to bond with the cows as naturally as if he had known them for years. Several days passed with him caring for the cows and even talking to them like they were his friends. Soon, his madness completely vanished and sanity returned. He continued living there with the newfound friends who had helped him recover. The cowshed became like a healing centre for many mentally challenged people. Just experiencing the natural love that the cows showered on their human friends rid many people of their mental fatigue and illnesses.

That's not all, some animal friends are trained to act as eyes for the blind, detect seizures and cancer (yes, cancer) and facilitate rehabilitation from debilitating illnesses. Feeling low and lonely? Keep that phone aside. Instead of checking your Twitter or Instagram, get your dog and go for a walk. The fresh air, meeting your neighbours and the exercise will do you a world of good and get you out of the blues. Are you a cat person? Playing with your cats can get your heart pumping and give you more energy. A true animal friend is bound to leave lasting paw prints all over your heart.

Let me tell you a moving story that went viral overnight on social media. It was a picture of a small boy holding a chicken in one hand (which he had accidentally run over and injured while he was cycling) while in the other hand, he held some money as he ran to a doctor to get the chicken proper treatment. It is commendable that the child had such great presence of mind and generosity, and it is heartening that so many people across the world appreciated the boy's large-heartedness.

Two herds of elephants in South Africa displayed some strange yet exemplary behaviour towards their human caretaker.* The herds of wild elephants walked

---

* 'Elephants Who Appeared To Mourn Their Human Friend Remain Protected', CBC, 25 July 2012, https://www.cbc.ca/strombo/news/saying-goodbye-elephants-hold-apparent-vigil-to-mourn-their-human-friend.ht

for at least twelve hours to reach the house of Anthony, a conservationist who had once saved their lives. Anthony had the unique gift of pacifying traumatized wild elephants and he had saved them from being shot by the Elephant Welfare Organization, who thought they were a danger to humans in the vicinity. Anthony had lived with the elephants and saved them from certain death. When he died, they travelled that great distance to come and bid farewell to the man they were grateful to. The mystery was, how did they know he had died? They arrived the day after Anthony died. They had not met him in eighteen months and had no knowledge of his whereabouts. Yet, they sensed that the man they so loved was about to die and had embarked on an arduous journey across many miles, guided purely by instinct, to his house to pay their last respects to him. They stayed there for two days and then returned to the wild. They never stopped being grateful to someone who saved their life and they grieved for him when he was gone.

What an example of friendship they set!

Gratitude, appreciation, respect and remembrance: all these values are personified by animals. They can teach us a thing or two about friendship if we're willing to learn. Try it for yourself.

Friendships Online

Technology has changed the world. Completely. What has also been affected is something as subtle as friendship. Online friendships are a whole new category of friendship in these times. The internet, a relatively new place to meet new people, continues to be a grey area when it comes to the quality of friendships one finds on it.

It's hard to keep up online friendships. It is so much more challenging to do all the things that you would do with your friends in real life. Going to the mall? Or going dancing together? But it turns out, online friendships can sometimes run deeper than real-world friendships. Sometimes, online friends meet and their friendship jumps from online to in-person, some even lasting for a long, long time. Or you can think of it as having friends in cool, faraway places you can visit at some point. Some people have been known to develop strong friendships and bonds online that have resulted in enduring real-life friendships and even marriages. The thing is that one should treat relationships online as only stepping stones towards deeper relationships, if at all. Only then do online relationships make sense. You have to understand that in the long term, a personal relationship is much more important and essential than an online relationship.

Many people tell me that in these relationships, they feel no one is judging them, either about their physical appearance or the way they talk. Fair enough, but how do you evaluate a friend? There's little information with which to truly evaluate somebody online. One always has to be cautious as there is no way to prove the authenticity of a person online. Safety remains an issue.

Another factor I've often wondered about myself is how would an online friend support you in ways other than giving just the virtual support on an online platform? In case one needs proximity and face-to-face conversation in person, who do you turn to? However, if you're lucky, when you need support, even your online friend might drop everything and come to help you, sometimes even across continents!

Do you think being online drives you to isolation or being isolated drives you online? Online friends are a boon for those who find it hard to interact with people in real life and feel like misfits. They find comfort in these friends they would have otherwise never met.

And last but not the least, does it hurt as much when you lose a friend online? Yes, it can, because you may have invested as much in the friendship and your emotions don't really differentiate between types of friends. Your ability to reason does that.

Online friendships just reinforce the fact that it is emotional connection that we humans crave and it is immaterial whether it is online, offline, terrestrial, celestial or even transcendental. Yes, we need transcendental connection too, with God, who commits himself as a suhrit or best friend to each and every living being. So go ahead, embrace the joy of friendship and give your friends new wings to fly with.

So although technology makes life so much easier, it poses certain challenges too. Let's have a quick look.

PRO—Internet gives us an opportunity to fill holes which cannot be filled by real-life friends. It's so much easier to find friends online who share common interests and can give advice on something that's embarrassing to bring up with personal friends.

CON—Emoticons don't always communicate the right emotions and typed words and lack of body language can convey the wrong meaning.

PRO—Giving opinions and sharing personal things are easier and comfortable with those who don't judge you or are prejudiced.

CON—Online friends can be deceptive or malicious and not necessarily committed in friendship. You never know who you are talking to. Catfishing (people pretending to be someone they are not) and adult predators are real concerns.

PRO—Introverts can shed their inhibitions and social anxiety behind the screen and come out of their shells.

CON—One can get addicted to social media and lose touch with reality. Social awkwardness creeps in. Affects physical and mental health adversely. Cyberbullying and stalking are known evils.

PRO—One can easily stop a conversation whenever one wishes to.

CON—An online friend can disappear overnight, causing an immense amount of emotional distress. This is one reason not to share personal data too soon and too readily.

PRO—Shy people, who otherwise have very few friends, can make online friends easily and not feel lonely.

CON—Can't go swimming or shopping together, can't hug either.

In short, although the internet allows great potential for the newest generation to make friends, changing the traditional concepts of friendship, one should be aware of the pitfalls too.

Now that you have finished reading the last chapter, I assume you have gained valuable insights into the world of friendship, be it friendship with others, your own self, parents, animals or online friends. Your friends, whoever they may be, will always make the world a more beautiful place to live in. I hope you will take up the mantle of doing right by your friends now, making the world more colourful for others as well, and sharing hope, joy, love and the dreams that make life a rainbow.

Summary:

- Different flavours of friendship include friendship with self, parents, online and with animals.
- Building a healthy intelligence and a strong value system helps forging friendship with oneself.
- Online friendships have their own pros and cons but they need to be treaded upon with utmost caution.

Activity

You think you know your friend well? Think of a friend you know well and answer these questions.

i.   Their favourite food _____

ii.   Their favourite restaurant _____

iii.   A phrase or word they use often_____

iv.   Favourite brand of clothes _____

v.   Favourite book _____

vi.   Favourite song or movie _____

vii.   Three words that best describe your friend _____

viii.   Person they are closest to in the family _____

ix.   What makes them most happy _____

x.   What makes them angry _____

xi.   Their greatest fear _____

To evaluate how well you know your friend, check your answers with them. Got a good score? Then you are truly a great friend. Got less than half right? You need to get to know your friend better!

Congratulations! I hope this book has helped you understand friendship a lot better and you can be a better friend to others as well as are able to assess who is a good friend to you. Based on such an understanding as offered in this book, I hope you could improve some of your relationships or if need be, decide to say goodbye to some others. Whatever the change in your equations with the people around you, don't forget to rearrange your Wheel of Friendship to reflect the change.

Date:

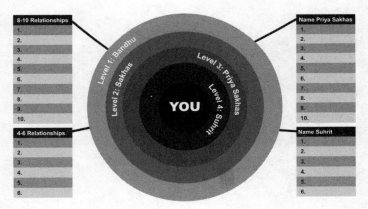

It has been a year since you last last analzyed the Wheel of Friendship. It's time to revisit your friendships once again!

Date:

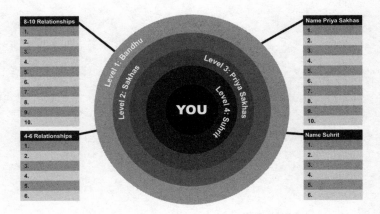

Acknowledgements

Here's to my friends who made me worthy of their friendship!

Two faces immediately crop up in my mind the moment I think of friendship—my best friends from school, Vibhav and Azhar. Whatever I am today, and whatever I achieve in life, they will have contributed to it to some extent. It was their love that shaped me in my formative years. The amazing bond that we shared became the foundation of my life.

My five closest friends from engineering college with whom I spent many wonderful moments need to be acknowledged. They showed me that life was beautiful when lived with love and harmony. Lenin, Dibin, Sydney, Rohan and Vibhav (again), the six of us made an inseparable bond that no amount of differences or distance could break. In addition to this gang of boys were some more amazing friends—Akshay, Shubhapriya, Sonia, Amareta, Valerie and Alzira—whose genuine love, faith and presence enhanced the meaning of true friendship in my life.

My understanding of friendship expanded infinitely in the eleven years I spent in the monastery, living as a monk amidst 150 other brilliant monks. Radheshlal, Rajgopal and Shadbhuj were three sincere, loving, genuine, intense and trusted friends who stood by me through thick and thin with no expectations whatsoever. We learnt, sang, danced, ate, meditated, studied and stayed together as friends, colleagues and spiritualists, all rolled into one.

I would also like to acknowledge the thousands of friends I have in every country across the world, who have continually shared their kindness and helped me develop a deeper conviction in the beauty of friendship.

Finally, my dear readers, I pray you develop faith in your friendships and experience the genuine love and warmth that only true friendship can generate.